FORGOTTEN WOMEN OF GOD

2013

*To Randle
with love for your
birthday.
May this book be
inspirational to you as
you have been to us.
Love,
Cheri & Craig*

*P.S. After you have read
this I would like to borrow
it back sometime to read
it. If that would be
OK.*

FORGOTTEN WOMEN OF GOD

Diana Webb

Illustrated by Diana Webb and Harold Petersen

Bonneville Books
Springville, Utah

© 2010 Diana Webb

All rights reserved.

No part of this book may be reproduced in any form whatsoever, whether by graphic, visual, electronic, film, microfilm, tape recording, or any other means, without prior written permission of the publisher, except in the case of brief passages embodied in critical reviews and articles.

This is not an official publication of The Church of Jesus Christ of Latter-day Saints. The opinions and views expressed herein belong solely to the author and do not necessarily represent the opinions or views of Cedar Fort, Inc. Permission for the use of sources, graphics, and photos is also solely the responsibility of the author.

ISBN 13: 978-1-59955-384-9

Published by Bonneville Books, an imprint of Cedar Fort, Inc., 2373 W. 700 S., Springville, UT 84663
Distributed by Cedar Fort, Inc., www.cedarfort.com

LIBRARY OF CONGRESS CATALOGING-IN-PUBLICATION DATA

Webb, Diana Barton.
 Forgotten Women of God / Diana Webb.
   p. cm.
  ISBN 978-1-59955-384-9
  1. Apocryphal books (Old Testament)--Criticism, interpretation, etc. 2. Women in the Bible. I. Title.

BS575.W38 2010
229.08'3054--dc22
                                    2009045360

Cover design by Angela D. Olsen
Cover design © 2010 by Lyle Mortimer
Edited and typeset by Katherine Carter
Printed in the United States of America

10 9 8 7 6 5 4 3 2 1

Printed on acid-free paper

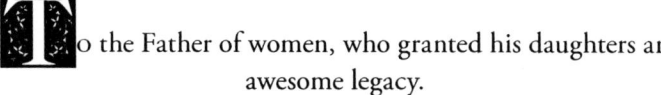o the Father of women, who granted his daughters an awesome legacy.

CONTENTS

Preface	ix
Introduction: What Are the Pseudepigrapha, Anyway?	xiii
1. Eve's Legacy: A Power Equal to Man	1
2. Susanna: Virtue over Villainy	7
3. Judith: Losing Your Head to a Beautiful Girl	21
4. Aseneth: Wife of Joseph and Paragon of Proselytes	35
5. New Girls on the Block	49
6. Seila: A Willing Sacrifice	77
7. The Women Who Rescued Moses	87
8. Deborah and Jael: "Into the Hand of a Woman"	105
9. Hannah: Silent No Longer	119
10. Hagar: Not Forgotten by God	137
11. Tamar: Maligned and Misunderstood	149
Conclusion	161
Glossary	165
About the Author	169

PREFACE

I HAVE ALWAYS LOVED THE scriptures. When I was a little girl, my Grandma Barton gave me a four-volume set of children's Bible stories from the Old Testament. They had brown leather spines with gold letters. They were not like today's children's stories with lots of colored pictures and large type. These stories had no colored pictures and were typeset in a small font. Instead, they contained beautiful woodcuts that conjured magical scenes in my young imagination. I was amazed that Samson could bring down an entire temple on the heads of the Philistines. I was fascinated by the giant hailstones that fell from the sky during the destruction of the armies of the Amorites, and I was engrossed by the countless drowned bodies of the Egyptians and their horses after the Red Sea came crashing down on them. I remember wondering at the depiction of Moses as he came down off Mount Sinai with light emanating from his head like horns.

One night, as my husband and I were enjoying dinner with another couple, our friend kept relating absorbing stories about people from the Bible that I had never heard of before. At least, they weren't in *my* Bible. I asked him where he had heard them, and he said that they came from the Old Testament pseudepigrapha—books that never made it into the biblical canon. These stories intrigued me, and the possibility that I might discover other engaging tales aroused my curiosity. The next week, I searched out and purchased a two-volume set of the pseudepigrapha edited by James H. Charlesworth and began dabbling in a new world of heretofore-undiscovered treasures.

When the last of my children entered school, I treated myself to classes held at the University of Utah Institute of Religion twice a week. The semester following my discovery of the pseudepigrapha, I went to the institute every day and took as many classes as I could before my children came home from school. I also attended a Friday morning adult religion class held at my church's meetinghouse. I was thrilled to be learning so much.

After several years of this, I was dismayed to find I had taken all of the classes that were offered at the institute. However, the next year the institute was offering a biblical Hebrew class, so I decided to sign up. In my previous classes, I had often heard my teachers say, "In Hebrew this means such and such," and I had often thought to myself, "How do I know if that's really true?" I had no way to check the translations. Was I cynical? Maybe I just had an inquiring mind.

As I started my new class, I was fascinated by all of the nuances of words in the scriptures that opened themselves up to me because I now understood their Hebrew roots. I loved discovering that *Elohim* was a plural word, and so meant "gods," not just "God." I loved learning that *Adam* could mean "first blood," because *aleph*, the first letter of the Hebrew alphabet, could also be used as the number one, and *dam* meant "blood." These were just the start of my discoveries. Things got a little dicey when we started learning Hebrew verb conjugations. I thought I would faint the day we learned that when a *vav* (the letter for *v* and the word for *and*) appears at the beginning of a sentence, the tense of the verb reverts to the opposite of what is written. Present tense becomes past, and past tense becomes present. I thought, "What? You've got to be kidding. How crazy can a language be?" But I loved it and hung in there.

One day I heard about a master's program at Brigham Young University called Master of Ancient Near Eastern Studies. When I read the requirements and the fields of study that would be explored, I was so excited! To be accepted, a student had to be able to read the Bible in Hebrew, so I signed up for Readings in the Hebrew Old Testament at BYU and took the Graduate Record Examination. Amazingly, I was accepted into the program! We had to immediately choose a topic for our thesis and write a prospectus. I decided to write about all of the women in the pseudepigrapha but ended up just focusing on the matriarchs—Eve, Sarah, Rebecca, Rachel, and Asenath. It was titled "Portrayal of the Matriarchs in the Old Testament pseudepigrapha." How's that for a snoozer? But I wasn't snoozing. I loved these Old Testament women.

Collected here are some of the stories of the fascinating but neglected women who populate the pages of the pseudepigrapha and the Apocrypha. You might already be acquainted with some of them, but you might discover that you didn't know them as well as you thought you did. Some will be completely new to you. I've loved meeting these Old Testament women, and I hope that others will as well.

INTRODUCTION
What Are the Pseudepigrapha, Anyway?

BEFORE JUMPING INTO THE TALES of the women in the Apocrypha and pseudepigrapha, a little background information might help. "The" Apocrypha (with the definite article) is a group of books that formed an integral part of the King James Bible when it was translated into English in A.D. 1611. All of the preceding English versions of the Bible since 1382 had also included these books, but they were seldom printed as part of it afterward. This is partially because the Puritans disapproved of them and began to drop them from their printings of the Geneva Bible, and it is also partly because contemporary Bible scholars discredit them because they were not part of the Hebrew Bible. Nevertheless, they were part of the Bible used by the early Christian church, which used the Greek translation of the Old Testament.[1]

First, let us look at the word *apocrypha* as it is a word that is greatly misunderstood. It comes from Greek and is formed from the combination of *apo* (away) and *kryptein* (hide or conceal). Thus, it signifies that which is "hidden away" or "concealed." *Apocryphon* is the singular form and *apocrypha* the plural. These words are used to describe the nature of a certain body of ancient religious writings.[2]

The word *apocrypha*, like many other words, has undergone a major change in meaning throughout the centuries. With regard to these ancient books, the word *apocrypha* originally meant a text too sacred and secret to be in everyone's hands. It needed to be hidden away and reserved for the spiritually mature. It was a term of dignity and respect. To those who revered the apocryphal books, they were "hidden" because they contained teachings that were too sacred to be revealed except to the initiated.[3] Others held the opposite view and thought these books should be hidden away because they were fraudulent or unorthodox. These writers applied the word *apocryphal* to works withheld from the public circulation—not because of their great worth, but because their value was secondary or questionable. After about three centuries of transition, the word *apocryphal* eventually gained an unfavorable connotation of being "false," "spurious," or "heretical." Thus, the word has acquired both a reputable connotation as well as a disparaging one, depending upon who is using it.[4]

The other term I should define is the word *canon*. It comes from the Hebrew word *kanah*, which means "reed." Reeds were originally used as measuring sticks. Thus, *canon* designates the "standard" or the "rule." Canonical works are those deemed reliable as statements of doctrine and faith.

As Robert J. Matthews explains, apocryphal literature is therefore called "non-canonical" or "extra-canonical." The Apocrypha (with the definite article and a capital *a*), Matthews writes, is generally used to refer to the fourteen additional books that are included with the Old Testament in many Bibles. The Greek Old Testament, or Septuagint, contains these books as does the Latin Bible used by the Catholic Church. Although Hebrew versions of the Apocrypha are not part of the Jewish Old Testament, they were accepted by the Hellenistic (or Greek-speaking) Jews, as evidenced by their inclusion in the Septuagint translation. By the fourth century, Christianity seemed to have accepted these books as canonical.[5]

Besides these books, there are numerous other books of Jewish and, sometimes, Christian authorship dating from the same period (200 B.C. to A.D. 100) that various groups of Jews and Christians received with respect. These writings, known as the pseudepigrapha, are often attributed to ideal figures in Israel's past such as Solomon, Abraham, or Adam. Among others, the pseudepigrapha include books known as Enoch, Jubilees, Joseph and Aseneth, and Testament of the Twelve Patriarchs.[6] The term *pseudepigrapha* is a transliteration of a Greek plural noun that means "with false superscription."

James Charlesworth contends that "many authors of [pseudepigraphal books] believed that they were recording God's infallible words. Early communities, both Jewish and Christian, took some pseudepigrapha very seriously."[7] The author of Jude quoted as prophecy a portion of First Enoch, which was recovered in Aramaic from one of the caves that contained the Dead Sea scrolls. Jude also refers several times to a Jewish writing about Moses that has been lost.[8]

The pseudepigrapha characteristically claim to contain God's words or messages and frequently build upon ideas and narratives present in the Old Testament. They are valuable to scholars and other truth seekers because they preserve Jewish traditions that date from that period (200 B.C. to A.D. 100).[9]

Charlesworth further explains, "It seems to follow, therefore, both that the early pseudepigrapha were composed during a period in which the limits of the canon apparently remained fluid at least to some Jews, and that some Jews and Christians inherited and passed on these documents as inspired. They did not necessarily regard them as apocryphal, or outside the canon."[10] Among many groups of Jews, this esoteric literature was as highly or more highly treasured than so-called "canonical" books.[11]

To say simply that the formation of the Old and New Testament canons was a long and complicated process that went through many phases is a gross understatement. It is difficult to ascertain what determined whether church officials regarded a book as inspired or not, and at times the designations they made seem almost arbitrary. Nonetheless, after a period of several centuries, they reached a certain degree of agreement. The first stage of this winnowing process was the growth and formation of the Hebrew canon.[12]

The Hebrew Bible is divided into three sections: the Law, the Prophets, and the Writings. The Law, which includes the five books of Moses, was accepted as canonical by the time the Jews returned from the Babylonian Captivity in the fifth century B.C. The Prophets, which includes the "former" prophets (Joshua, Judges, Samuel, and Kings) and the "latter" prophets (Isaiah, Jeremiah, Ezekiel, and the twelve minor prophets) was considered "scripture" by the second century B.C. The books in the Writings were the last section of the Hebrew Bible to be recognized as canonical. This group includes Psalms, Proverbs, Job, the Song of Songs, Esther, Ruth, Ecclesiastes, Ezra, Nehemiah, and Chronicles.[13]

The council of Jamnia convened to select these books in western Judea in about A.D. 90. The council became necessary when new sacred writings authored by Jewish Christians appeared. At first both Jews and Gentiles regarded the Christian church as merely another Jewish sect that followed a prophet named Jesus. These Christians accepted the Jewish Old Testament, but when they came out with what they claimed as their own authoritative documents (writings in addition to the Old Testament), the Jewish leaders realized they had a problem. They did not want to be associated with these Christian ideas and writings, so they sought a way to distance themselves from Christianity. They reacted by creating their own list of canonical books, which, of course, did not include the Christian books. They not only rejected the Christian writings by people such as Matthew, Peter, John, and others, but (in examining the books of the Old Testament) they also struggled with their doubts about other books. They wondered if the Song of Solomon (Song of Songs) had any spiritual value, but they finally accepted it as an allegory of God's love for the house of Israel. The thirty-nine books that were finally pronounced canonical had been so highly regarded by Jewish people that the Jewish Council at Jamnia merely ratified what had been agreed upon by "long and approved usage" of the books.[14]

During the long period in which the Hebrew scriptures were compiled, Jewish authors were producing other books. Some of these books are mentioned in the scriptural canon. We are asked in Judges, "Is this not written in the Book of Jasher?" We are also told repeatedly to consult the "Chronicles of the Kings of Israel." None of these texts is known to exist today, probably because no one esteemed them enough to copy and recopy them for posterity. In contrast, the existing books of the Apocrypha and pseudepigrapha apparently *were* considered worthy of being recopied for future generations. Undoubtedly, there was a period in which their value was being appraised, along with some of the later books for inclusion in the Writings section in the Hebrew Bible.[15]

In A.D. 1546, the Roman Catholic Church declared certain apocryphal books to be inspired and "on a par with the books of the Old Testament."[16] These included certain supplements to the books of Daniel and Esther, Tobit, Judith, Ecclesiasticus, Wisdom, Baruch and 1 and 2 Maccabees. This resulted in a significant difference between how the books were arranged in the copies of the Old Testament prepared for the Catholic Church and those prepared for Protestant churches. In the Catholic versions of the Bible, the books were *interspersed* among the books of the Old Testament, since all were considered to be canonical. In Protestant Bibles, the apocryphal books appear in a separate block at the end of the Old Testament, showing that they were regarded as sacred writings, but not on par with the Old Testament canon and, in time, they were omitted completely. The title page of a Catholic Bible states that it contains the Old and New Testaments. The rare Protestant Bible that still contains the Apocrypha has a title page stating that the book contains the Old and New Testaments "and the Apocrypha."

The process of canonization is a long and complicated story. We don't know just when and why certain books became regarded as authoritative. Clearly it was a gradual process that progressed subtly and sometimes imperceptibly until certain books emerged as the recognized word of God.

Even though many accounts of ancient women in the Bible are brief, expanded versions of these stories can be found in pseudepigraphical and rabbinic commentary as well as in the Targums of the Old Testament. When the Jews returned from the Babylonian captivity to rebuild their temple in Jerusalem, they spoke the *lingua franca* of Babylon, which was Aramaic. Although Aramaic was a cousin to Hebrew, they could no longer understand the Hebrew scriptures when the scribes read aloud to them. The scribes had to explain the meaning of the Hebrew words to the people, and their interpretations reflect the way people understood the scriptures at the time. These explanations were called Targums and were written down and collected during the following centuries.

Although these additions to the scriptures are not canonical, they often reflect the accepted theology and Jewish traditions of ancient times. I personally love gaining new insights into the lives of the "forgotten" women found in these texts. I am blown away by the strength these amazing women possessed, and their examples have given me a new awareness of my role as a woman.

Notes

1. Edgar J. Goodspeed, *The Apocrypha: An American Translation* (New York: Vintage Books, 1989), v.

2. Robert J. Matthews, "Whose Apocrypha?" in *Apocryphal Writings and the Latter-day Saints* (Provo: Religious Studies Center, 1986), 2–3.

3. Ibid., 3.

4. Bruce M. Metzger, *An Introduction to the Apocrypha* (New York: Oxford University Press, 1957), 5.

5. Matthews, "Whose Apocrypha?" in *Apocryphal Writings and the Latter-day Saints*, 3–4.

6. Metzger, *An Introduction to the Apocrypha*, 7.

7. James H. Charlesworth, *The Old Testament Pseudepigrapha*, vol. 2 (Garden City: Doubleday, 1985), xxii.

8. Ibid., xxiv.

9. Ibid., xxv.

10. Ibid., xxii.

11. R. H. Charles, *The Apocrypha and Pseudepigrapha of the Old Testament*, vol. 2 (London: Oxford University Press, 1913), vii.

12. Metzger, *An Introduction to the Apocrypha*, 6–7.

13. Ibid., 7–8.

14. Ibid., 8.

15. Ibid., 8–9.

16. Ibid., 6.

CHAPTER 1

Eve's Legacy: A Power Equal to Man
Genesis 2:18

WHAT CAN WE LEARN FROM the stories of ancient women as they are portrayed in extracanonical writings and in the Bible? Do these ancient writings have any relevance for women in our century? Can we find any new role models within these pages?

For years we have accepted the "virtuous woman" of Proverbs 31:10 as the ideal we should emulate—never letting our candles go out and spinning and toiling for our husbands and children. Sometimes this seems out of touch with the challenges faced by the women of today's world. As Carolyn Curtis James points out in *Lost Women of the Bible*, most of the stories in the Bible follow the "wife and mother" model and reinforce the idea that God most often does his work through men.[1] When women in the Bible don't fit into the wife and mother definition, they experience great personal pain and social ostracism. Other biblical women fit this model at first and have seemingly ideal lives until the premature death of a husband causes them to be at the mercy of a society where they no longer fit in.

When I first pondered these questions, I was impressed to consider what vision God had in mind for women when he created Eve. Although the Bible strongly validates the role of women as wives and mothers, it also shows that "God values us just as much when our lives follow other paths."[2] As I searched the library shelves for books about the role of women in God's plan, I was amazed with the vast body of literature that has been published in the last fifteen years since I researched for my master's thesis. A whole new generation of female Bible scholars has emerged that has greatly enriched our understanding of the scriptures. Women bring different questions as well as different points of view as they consider the stories from the scriptures.[3] Maybe that's because women really are from "Venus" and most biblical points of view come from male-oriented "Mars." For whatever reason it is that men and women tend to see things differently, women scholars have pointed out new facets of ancient stories that we had overlooked before.

When I was first learning to read Genesis 2:18 in Hebrew, I noticed a lot of things I had not noticed in past readings. Woman is not created at the same time as man but only *after* God has created Adam. Some people may use this to explain why many of Eve's modern descendants tend to be late for social gatherings, but it actually has much deeper significance. Before Eve's creation, God concludes that it is not good for man to be alone. The text reads: "And the Lord God said, it is not good that the man should be alone, [therefore] I will make him a help meet for him." After God repeats seven times that the newly created earth and everything on it is "good," we are suddenly informed that it is "not good" that man be alone. It is not just less than optimal; it is in complete opposition to the way God is used to doing things.[4] This is startling news indeed. Something is terribly wrong with man being alone.

Anciently, aloneness was viewed as the "negation of authentic living, for true life is not individual but corporate and social."[5] So, now that we know man needs woman, what exactly is a "help meet"? I had learned to understand these archaic English words as "helpmate." The woman is supposed to be a helper suitable for the man. I thought it meant that woman is supposed to make man's dinner and hand him the wrench when he is fixing the car. *Helper* has the connotation in English of an assistant of lesser status.

That is not at all what these words are intended to convey. "Help meet for him" in Hebrew is *ezer kenegdo*. As I studied the definitions of these words, I found that they actually meant something very different from what I had understood for years. When God decided to create another creature so that man would not be alone, he did not merely make a helper for him—he made an equal partner. David Freedman writes that these words should be translated as "a power equal to man."[6]

The Hebrew noun *ezer* (pronounced ay-zer) describes an equal if not a superior. *Ezer* in the Old Testament is most frequently used to describe how God is an *ezer* to man. It definitely does *not* have the connotation of a mere "helper" in any of the cases in which it is used. A more accurate translation would be a "power" or "strength."

Etymological evidence indicates that *ezer* originally had two roots, one *-z-r*, meaning "to rescue" or "to save," and the other *g-z-r*, meaning "to be strong."[7] The related verb *azar* means "to succor, to save from extremity, and to deliver from death." It refers to the actions of one who gives water to someone dying of thirst, thus saving his life. Samuel Terrien argues that, "Far from being a subordinated or menial servant, woman is the savior of man."[8] Women may have believed this for centuries, but now a man is actually affirming it in print. Donna B. Nielsen notes that *ezer* possesses a wide range of ideas including royalty, rigor, courage, efficiency, and adventurousness. The root of the verb calls to mind achievement, pioneering, and risk taking.[9]

Each of these ancient roots, *-z-r* and *g-z-r*, began with a different Hebrew guttural sound. Some ancient languages made a distinction between the two letters and others did not. Hebrew no longer distinguishes between them. Around 1500 B.C. these two different sounds began to be written with the same sign. Later the two pronunciations also merged. As a result, when the Bible was written, what had once been two roots of *ezer* had merged into one. With the merger of pronunciation and writing came the merger of meanings. Thus, *ezer* could mean both "to be strong" and "to save." In time the root was always interpreted as "to help" which was a mixture of the nuances of both meanings.[10] And I thought high school English was challenging!

The second word that caught my attention in the Hebrew of Genesis 2:18 was the word *kenegdo*, which traditionally has been translated as "meet for" or "fit for." Because *kenegdo* appears only once in the

Bible, scholars had little upon which to base their translations. *Neged*, a related word which means "against," was one of the first words I learned in Hebrew. I thought it was very strange that God would create a companion for Adam that was "against" him! Later, I learned that *kenegdo* could also mean "in front of" or "opposite."[11] This still didn't help that much. Finally I heard it explained as being "exactly corresponding to," like when you look at yourself in a mirror.

In Mishnaic Hebrew, the root *kened* means "equal."[12] The King James translation of *kenegdo* for "meet for" is based on the seventeenth-century meaning of "meet" as "worthy of," which has long been out of current usage. This archaic translation has led to the formation of the word "help-meet" to describe a good wife, although nobody really knew how this was different than "helpmate." Any way you look at it, the meaning intended by the original Hebrew was totally lost. Good wives all want to be "helpmates" but completely miss the fact that the scripture clearly teaches that God created woman to be an equal partner to her husband, exactly corresponding to him in every way.

The noun *ezer* occurs twenty-one times in the Hebrew Bible. In eight of these instances, the word means "savior." These examples are easy to identify because they are associated with other expressions of deliverance or saving. Elsewhere in the Bible, the root *ezer* means "strength."[13]

In 1 Samuel 7:12, Samuel erects a stone to commemorate the help God has given Israel in its victory over the fierce Philistines. In Hebrew, "stone" is *eben* and "help" is *ezer*, hence the stone is called Eben-ezer.[14] This monument seems like a nice gesture—a sort of ancient plaque to help remember the help that God gave in battle. However, if we look at the story a little closer, we see that God has given a little more than ordinary "help." I would define "ordinary" help as maybe God strengthening the Israelites to be at the top of their game when fighting their enemies. But this is quite a bit more than a little boost in strength. If we back up a couple of verses and look at 1 Samuel 7:10, we find this: "And as Samuel was offering up the burnt offering, the Philistines drew near to battle against Israel: but the Lord thundered with a great thunder on that day upon the Philistines, and discomfited them; and they were smitten before Israel." After dedicating the battle to the Lord, the armies of Israel sat back and watched as the Philistines were given a huge dose of divine "special effects." During the battle itself, the Lord demonstrated that he was fighting for Israel as he called the elements of nature into service. The thundering from heaven threw the enemy into confusion, striking a "holy terror" into them. I think I would use the term "rescue" or "deliverance" rather than the rather anemic "help" as it is translated in 1 Samuel.

However, I must admit that the word "help" is anything *but* anemic at times. When the house is burning down, you have fallen down a well unseen, or you are hanging on to the edge of a cliff with your fingernails, what is the one word that you scream at the top of your lungs? *HELP!* At these times you want all the strength, power, and deliverance you can muster!

God, knowing that Adam couldn't fight the battles of earth life alone, created a companion for him who would fulfill both of these meanings of *ezer*. Woman would be a "strength" to him in helping meet all the challenges that earth-life would launch—pain, toil, discouragement, rebellion, burnout, and faltering faith. At times she might even "rescue" him with precious insights into the meaning of their trials, or "save" him from discouragement or despair. As Carolyn Curtis James has asserted, God created woman to be an *ezer* to man. To strengthen *and* to save. Woman is his greatest ally. This is Eve's legacy for all women, not just within the bonds of marriage, but wherever she touches the lives of others in the world at large.[15]

Recently my niece was married in Arizona, and all my siblings gathered at my sister's house to attend. It was fun to be together under one roof, and we enjoyed the camaraderie. We got up early and enjoyed cooking, eating, and talking. One morning my sister-in-law came down after nine o'clock, and my brother was giving her a hard time. "Up at the crack of nine, huh? What have you been doing?" She answered coolly. "Oh, I've just been saving the world. All of my kids called and needed me to solve their problems." Everybody laughed at her supposedly sarcastic remark. But as I thought about it, she wasn't too far from the truth. She *was* saving the world—at least, her little corner of it, anyway. She was fulfilling her divine calling as an *ezer*, a rescuer. Her help and advice was indispensable to her children.

I have chosen to write about some of the little-known women from the Bible and other ancient writings that have lived up to Eve's legacy as *ezers*. In the chapters that follow, I hope that we can examine these women as *ezers* and identify their qualities of strength and their roles as rescuers.

Notes

1. Carolyn Curtis James, *Lost Women of the Bible* (Grand Rapids: Zondervan, 2005), 18.

2. Ibid., 20.

3. Ibid., 21.

4. Gordon J. Wenham, *Word Biblical Commentary*, vol. 1, (Waco: Word Books, 1987), 68.

5. Samuel Terrien, *Till the Heart Sings: A Biblical Theology of Manhood and Womanhood* (Philadelphia: Fortress Press, 1985), 9.

6. R. David Freeman, "Woman, a Power Equal to Man," *Biblical Archaeology Review*, Jan/Feb 1983, 56.

7. Ibid.

8. Terrien, *Till the Heart Sings: A Biblical Theology of Manhood and Womanhood*, 10.

9. Donna B. Nielsen, *Beloved Bridegroom* (Provo: Onyx Press, 1999), 8.

10. Freeman, "Woman, a Power Equal to Man," 58.

11. Frances Brown, *The New Brown–Driver–Briggs–Gesenius Hebrew and English Lexicon* (Peabody: Hendrickson Publishers, 1979), 617.

12. The Mishnah is a major work of Rabbinic Judaism and the first major redaction into written form of Jewish oral traditions, called the Oral Torah. See glossary.

13. Freeman, "Woman, a Power Equal to Man," 56.

14. Many readers will be familiar with the beloved hymn "Come, Thou Fount of Every Blessing," which contains the line, "Here I raise my Ebenezer." Few understand that it refers to this story in 1 Samuel 7:12. (Text by Robert Robinson, 1758; Melody from John Wyeth's "Repository of Sacred Music.")

15. James, *Lost Women of the Bible*, 36–37.

CHAPTER 2

Susanna: Virtue over Villainy
The History of Susanna

FOR OVER TWENTY-TWO CENTURIES, READERS have taken delight in *The History of Susanna*, a short tale about a beautiful and pious woman who is encountered by two conniving villains that intend to satisfy their lust with her. She is saved by her own virtue—despite the threat of blackmail and death—and aided by the artful legal maneuvering of a young superstar named Daniel. There are at least one hundred thirty-seven major versions of the Susanna story in drama, fiction, poetry, and paintings.[1] It is the Bible's version of the damsel in distress tale. If you flip through your Bible in search of the Susanna story, however, you may be disappointed. Your Bible may not include her story at all. Susanna's story and its placement in the biblical canon is almost as interesting as the story itself.[2]

The History of Susanna is part of the additions to the Book of Daniel, three in number, along with *Bel and the Dragon* and *The Prayer of the Three Children*. Daniel is the story of a righteous young Jew living in exile in the land of Babylon. T. J. Wray writes that the focus of the book of Daniel is to encourage Jews to hold fast to their religion despite foreign domination and to resist the polluting influence of all other religions. *The History of Susanna* was added to the Greek translation of the Hebrew Bible, the Septuagint, made in the second century B.C. This may appear problematic, as it places the story long after the story of the Babylonian captivity, which took place between 587–539 B.C. Although this at first may seem to be a glaring error in the story, it is actually a rather common biblical convention. "Many, if not *most*, of the stories found in the Bible," Wray asserts, "were written long after the purported events took place, sometimes even hundreds of years later."[3]

Catholics accept Susanna's tale as part of the official canon, and it is found in the Catholic Bible as chapter thirteen of Daniel. *Susanna* is also part of the Apocrypha of the Old Testament in many Protestant Bibles, including the King James Translation. (All quotations used in this chapter are from that translation.) It is, however, not part of the Jewish canon, though Susanna is much admired among Jews as a paragon of faith and piety.[4] The sixty-four verses of this well-told story finely craft the theme of virtue triumphing over villainy.

The story of Susanna begins almost like a fairy tale: "There dwelt a man in Babylon, called Joacim: And he took a wife, whose name was Susanna, the daughter of Chelsias, a very fair woman, and one that feared the Lord. Her parents also were righteous, and taught their daughter according to the law of Moses" (1–3). This is a story of an exiled people in Babylon, endeavoring to remain faithful to their covenant with the God of Israel while living in surroundings hostile to their religion, culture, and traditions. We are told in the next line, however, that despite these obstacles, Joacim, Susanna's husband, is "a great rich man" (4) and enjoys a position of respect in the community. Their house is adjoined by a "fair garden" where the elders gather to consider points of the law. The exile in Babylon is a long one, and some of the Israelites have risen to positions of authority and prestige, adjusting well to the Babylonian lifestyle and culture while maintaining their own religious traditions and awaiting the time when they will be able to return home.[5]

As in most fairy tales, events soon take a drastic turn for the worse. Two lustful miscreants who are eager to carry out devilish designs appear on the scene: "The same year were appointed two of the ancients of the people to be judges . . . . These kept much at Joacim's house: and all that had any suits in law came unto them" (5–6). The judges are familiar with Susanna because of their visits to her husband's home and garden where she often walked. "Now when the people departed away at noon, Susanna went into her husband's garden to walk. And the two elders saw her going in every day, and walking; so that their lust was inflamed toward her" (7–8).

Each of the elders wallows in his own private passion for Susanna but each is embarrassed to reveal his lust. They separately watch her. "And they perverted their own mind, and turned away their eyes, that they might not look unto heaven, nor remember just judgments. And albeit they both were wounded with her love, yet durst not one shew another his grief. For they were ashamed to declare their lust, that they desired to have to do with her. Yet they watched diligently from day to day to see her" (9–12). Would watching "diligently" qualify as stalking, I wonder?

One day a comical but pathetic situation arises. After a day at court, the elders say to each other, "Let us now go home: for it is dinner time" (13). They each leave, pretending to be going home to dinner. They circle around to the garden, hoping to catch a glimpse of Susanna, but they accidentally bump into each other instead. After they each ask what the other is doing there, they both admit their lust for Susanna. As if it isn't bad enough to harbor feelings of lechery toward a respected community member's wife, the judges now enter into a degenerate conspiracy to approach her together in order to have their way with her.

The two fiendish villains bide their time, awaiting the perfect moment to approach her. "And it fell out, as they watched a fit time, she went in as before with two maids only, as she was desirous to wash herself in the garden: for it was hot. And there was no body there save the two elders, that hid themselves, and watched her" (15–16). Susanna then sends her maids away to fetch oil and washing balls and tells them to shut the garden doors behind them. She is so modest she does not feel comfortable bathing in the presence of her own maids. After they leave, the two elders spring from their hiding places. They accost Susanna in her bath and attempt to threaten her into letting them have their way with her, saying, "Behold, the garden doors are shut, that no man can see us, and we are in love with thee: therefore consent unto us, and lie with us. If thou wilt not, we will bear witness against thee, that a young man was with thee: and therefore thou didst send away thy maids from thee" (20–21).

Susanna knows that she is caught in a trap. If she refuses the elders, they will falsely testify of her adultery and she will be executed. The penalty for adultery is death, according to the law of Moses.[6] They are "respected" elders, and Susanna is a woman. In biblical times, a woman's testimony was considered unreliable in court proceedings, so the magistrates will probably triumph.[7] Recognizing what is at stake, she courageously replies, "I am straitened on every side: for if I do this thing, it is death unto me: and if I do it not, I cannot escape your hands. It is better for me to fall into your hands, and not do it, than to sin in the sight of the Lord" (22–23). Susanna then cries "with a loud voice" (24), and the two elders shout accusations at her. The servants, hearing the shrieking in the garden, return to see what is going on. They are dismayed to see Susanna in such a compromised position. When the elders make their allegations, the servants are astonished, "for there was never such a report made of Susanna" (27).

After this the action moves quickly. The next day there is a meeting in Joacim's house, and the two elders come also "full of mischievous imagination against Susanna to put her to death" (28). She is summoned and arrives with her parents, children, and relatives. Curiously absent from this list of supporters is her husband, Joacim. T. J. Wray speculates about why: Does Joacim "recuse himself from the proceedings because of his personal involvement with the defendant? Is he too upset to watch the proceedings? Or, does his absence indicate that perhaps he himself believes Susanna is guilty?"[8]

Susanna is veiled, but the elders force her to remove her veil, "that they might be filled with her beauty" (32). When her friends and the others present see her in such a humiliated condition, they weep, for Susanna is "a very delicate woman, and beauteous to behold" (31). To oblige Susanna to unveil under such circumstances is a great indignity, according to Near Eastern thought. Culturally, it approaches symbolic rape.[9] In an alternate translation of this story found in the Septuagint, Susanna is forced to remove *all* of her clothes and stand before the court naked.[10]

Before anyone even questions Susanna, the two elders have the audacity to lay their hands upon her head to pronounce her guilt. The laying on of hands is a legal formality prescribed in ancient Jewish courts. However, it is ordinarily a sign from a witness that the accused is worthy of death, as illustrated in Leviticus 24:14: "Bring forth him that hath cursed without the camp; and let all that heard him lay their hands upon his head, and let all the congregation stone him." The laying on of the elders' hands before examination is a red flag that the jury may be fixed and that the chief witnesses—in fact the only witnesses—are also the lawyers who have already determined the final outcome of the case.

The elders' actions ironically mirror another levitical act. When someone sacrificed an animal, he laid his hands upon the animal's head to transfer his sins from himself to the animal. Leviticus 1:4 states, "And he shall put his hand upon the head of the burnt offering; and it shall be accepted for him to make atonement for him." Susanna is going like a lamb to the slaughter, the sins of the elders being vicariously thrust upon her.[11] And yet Susanna does not give up hope that these two seemingly upstanding members of society will, in the end, receive what they deserve from the source of ultimate justice. "And she weeping looked up toward heaven: for her heart trusted in the Lord" (35).

The two villains recite their manufactured story: "As we walked in the garden alone, this woman came in with two maids, and shut the garden doors, and sent the maids away. Then a young man, who there was hid, came unto her, and lay with her. Then we that stood in a corner of the garden, seeing this wickedness, ran unto them. And when we saw them together, the man we could not hold: for he was stronger than we, and opened the door, and leaped out. But having taken this woman, we asked who the young man was, but she would not tell us: these things we do testify" (36–40).

Astonishingly, the assembly believes the testimony of the elders, and Susanna is sentenced to death. This society takes the word of a man—especially an elder—over the word of a woman. And with the testimony of *two* elders against her, Susanna does not stand a chance. She has no one to turn to but the Lord, and she cries out with a loud voice, "O everlasting God, thou knowest the secrets, and knowest all things before they be: Thou knowest that they have borne false witness against me, and, behold, I must die; whereas I never did such things as these men have maliciously invented against me" (42–43). Susanna has faith that God does not allow the wicked to escape justice. In the next verse we are told, "And the Lord heard her voice," as he hears the voices of all those who are unjustly accused and who are oppressed for their righteousness.

As Susanna is being taken away for execution, "the Lord [raises] up the holy spirit of a young youth," whose name is Daniel (45). He cries with a loud voice, "I am clear from the blood of this woman" (46), refusing to participate in her death. Standing in the midst of the people, he boldly addresses them: "Are ye such fools, ye sons of Israel, that without examination or knowledge of the truth ye have condemned a daughter of Israel? Return again to the place of judgment: for they have borne false witness against her" (48–49). The people return to the house of Joacim with Daniel. He asks that the elders be separated from each other so that he might question them individually and be able to detect any inconsistencies in their testimonies.

Daniel begins his interrogation by castigating the elders' behavior, their practiced pretense, and their degenerate morality. He says: "Now thy sins which thou hast committed aforetime are come to light: For thou hast pronounced false judgment, and hast condemned the innocent, and hast let the guilty go free; albeit the Lord saith, The innocent and righteous shalt thou not slay" (52–53). He asks the first elder the location of the alleged love nest: "If thou hast seen her, tell me, under what tree sawest thou them companying together?" The elder answers, "Under a mastick tree" (54). When Daniel asks the second elder the same question, the elder answers, "Under a holm tree" (58). Although they testify that they were together when they witnessed it, the elders have tripped over their words and revealed discrepancies between their accounts. Daniel cries, "Well; thou hast lied against thine own head" (55), and says that "the angel of God waiteth with the sword to cut thee in two, that he may destroy you" (59). Daniel claims victory and becomes the Perry Mason of his time.

The people then turn against the elders and condemn them to death, "for Daniel had convicted them of false witness by their own mouth" (61). "And according to the law of Moses they did unto them in such sort as they maliciously intended to do to their neighbor: and they put them to death" by beheading (62). The story seems to end happily-ever-after: "Thus the innocent blood was saved the same day. Therefore Chelsias and his wife praised God for their daughter Susanna, with Joacim her husband, and all the kindred, because there was no dishonesty found in her. From that day forth was Daniel had in great reputation in the sight of the people" (62–64).

The humiliating placing of the elders' hands on Susanna's head prefigures their own humiliation in amazingly literal ways. Susanna cries, "I cannot escape your hands" (22) and sadly concludes "it is better that I fall into your hands" (23). When Daniel announces the fate of the elders, he uses words that call back the placing of their defiled hands on Susanna's innocent head: "Thou hast lied against thine own head" (55). The importance in the story of hands and heads might clarify why Daniel sentences these two miscreants to beheading rather than to the traditional stoning that would have normally been prescribed for their false witness.[12]

This tale, which is a masterpiece of brevity, raises many questions in the mind of the modern reader. Several such questions are listed here from Steven C. Walker's book *Seven Ways of Looking at Susanna*:

> How does Daniel know Susanna to be innocent? Why do neither Susanna's husband nor her family nor her friends defend her? What makes the elders think they can get away with their gross miscarriage of justice? Why is the assembly so readily taken in by their deception? How does the young Daniel master sufficient social weight as a stranger in this tight-knit community to reverse its judicial decision? Why is the assembly so easily swayed to contradict its initial judgment?[13]

Clearly, as Walker points out, this is a story of reversals. The people "arose against the two elders" (61) just as they formerly "rose up" (19) against Susanna. The narrative dramatically illustrates the community's reversal in attitude toward the two elders, changing from resounding approval—"all that had any suits in law came unto them" (6)—to rousing disapproval—"they put them to death" (62).[14]

The History of Susanna is fraught with legal allusions: Daniel's name means "God is my judge," Susanna is taught according to the law of Moses, and her husband's home is a place of judgment and legal affairs. This brief tale contains not just the account of one trial, but two—the elders' as well as Susanna's. The heroic Daniel is both a defense attorney and a prosecuting attorney. The scoundrels are first prosecuting attorneys, then witnesses, and then defendants themselves. And as the meaning of Daniel's name insinuates, this story is ultimately about the trials of character that will be judged by the Supreme Judge of all judges.

Susanna is a parable about witnessing—not only in the verbal sense of "testifying," but also in the experiential sense of "seeing." Both meanings are critical to the legal issues of the story. No matter how long the elders "watched diligently . . . to see" (12), they are shortsighted because they only feel concern for themselves. From this limited perspective, they "perverted their own mind and turned away their eyes, that they might not look unto heaven" (9). In contrast, Susanna, though her eyes are clouded by tears, is able to look "up toward heaven" (35) and retain her trust in the Lord. The elders see the world in their own reflection. When they testify of "seeing this wickedness" (38) it is because that is all they are capable of seeing. When they try to convince Susanna that "no man can see us," (20) they reveal their moral shortsightedness. Susanna worships a God who sees all and "knowest the secrets" (42). She convinces all of us who have both eyes and voices that we also have a strong moral responsibility to "witness."[15]

At the center of the legal issues in *The History of Susanna* is the value and necessity of cross-examining witnesses. Young Daniel exposes the duplicity of the two elders through amazing legal acrobatics. The reader wonders how Daniel thinks to pose the questions he does. After all, why did the alleged love scene with the young man have to occur under a tree? How does he bait the elders into admitting they saw the seduction but did nothing to stop it until it was over? What were they looking at that they failed to identify the young man or restrain him even though they outnumbered him? Their credibility gradually begins to slip after each astute question Daniel asks. R. A. F. MacKenzie asserts that the main point of the story is that God confers on Daniel, his instrument of justice, "a supernatural knowledge of the truth." Perhaps his skill, or luck, is really a matter of divine influence as the text suggests—"The Lord raised up the holy spirit of a young youth, whose name was Daniel" (45). Or is it a combination of all of the above: divine inspiration, sound reasoning on Daniel's part, and extraordinary detective skills.[16]

In fact, it is Daniel's condemnation of the existing legal system that might have kept *The History of Susanna* from being authorized as scripture. The Hebrew canon, which was fixed in A.D. 90, would not have been popular with elders, and they were the ones who decided the new canon. They, obviously, would not want "elders" to come off looking shady. Also, the members of the Sanhedrin, which consisted of both Pharisees and Sadducees, would have differed in their interpretation of the law that condemned the elders to death. "Sadducean interpretation of the law would have let off the guilty Elders; but the Pharisaic principle is rigorously carried out in their execution."[17] This conflict between the two sects of elders could also have deterred the acceptance of the book.

The entire story of Susanna is understated but quietly compelling. Susanna bathes because "it was hot" (11). The real point of the nude scene may not be the sensuality of Susanna's flesh at all, nor the elders' reckless reaction to it, but the portrayal of her character. In contrast with celebrated heroines such as Judith or Jael, Susanna's passive resistance reveals her as the ultimate heroine for second century B.C. Jews and for us. Her statement that "It is better for me to fall into your hands, and not do it, than to sin in the sight of the Lord" (23) reveals her fearless faith. She is not afraid of what the elders can do to her, and she refuses to offend the Lord. The "most vividly understated" dimension of *The History of Susanna* is its characterization.[18]

Perhaps the most conspicuous lesson from *Susanna* is that things are not always as they seem. The actions of the two elders catch our attention as readers because they are so utterly despicable. What can motivate two respected elders—judges, even—to sink to spying and attempting a seduction in broad daylight? Worse still, they react to Susanna's refusal of their amorous advances with an attempt at legal murder. In other midrashic versions of the story, Susanna is but one object of the elders' carnal desire. This would explain why Daniel says: "O thou that are waxen old in wickedness" (52). The elders' technique seems far from suave as they proposition Susanna *together* and try to threaten her instead of persuade—two old men awkwardly snatching

15

a last chance at "love." The way they use this term, however, makes it easy to interchange with lust, as if they do not recognize any difference between the two.

The scene where the two elders bump into each other in the garden is even more amusing in the Septuagint version: "They came stealthily, evading each other, hurrying to see which should be first to show himself to her and to speak with her. And behold! she was taking her walk according to her wont and the one elder had barely arrived, when lo! the other came up. Then the one began to cross-examine his fellow, demanding, 'Why art thou gone forth so very early leaving me behind?' "(12–13).[19]

The elders seem to cease to exist as individual personalities but are both reduced to the common denominator of their shared lust. They do everything exactly alike, that is, until the moment they are questioned by Daniel and provide disastrously different responses. They have lost their perspective of reality and their ability to empathize with human emotion. Their lust has caused them to oversimplify their view of the world, seeing Susanna, not as another human being, but merely as an object to satisfy them sexually. They have already lost their souls long before they are condemned to die. They blame Susanna for their lust, as if to justify their murderous actions. Weighed down by ego, and their integrity dulled by past moral failings, the elders perceive Susanna as a temptation—a temptation they've lost the backbone to resist.[20]

Although Susanna is clearly an extremely good-looking woman, it seems equally clear that she is not aware of her beauty. Steven C. Walker writes that a person as reclusive and demure as Susanna would not risk bathing in the open if she realized how seductive her conduct might prove to be. If she is aware of her loveliness at all, she regards it of no consequence. It is only when she is accosted by the elders that she realizes her beauty might be a dubious asset.[21]

Susanna's rejection of the two elders calls to mind the classic biblical story of Joseph and Potiphar's wife in Genesis 39. Like Susanna, Joseph resists temptation on religious grounds. Being attracted by the handsome young Joseph, Potiphar's wife begs him day after day to lie with her, but each time "he hearkened not unto her" (Genesis 39:10). In answer to her pleas he says, "There is none greater in this house than I; neither hath [Potiphar] kept back any thing from me but thee, because thou art his wife: how then can I do this great wickedness, and sin against God?" (Genesis 39:9). This response is almost an exact corollary to Susanna's response to the elders when accosted by them: "It is better for me to fall into your hands, and not do it, than to sin against God" (23). St. Chrystostom compares the two seduction attempts:

> Susanna endured a severe fight, more severe than Joseph. He, a man, contended with one woman; but Susanna, a woman, had to contend with two men, and was a spectacle to men and to angels. The slander against her fidelity to her marriage-vow, the fear of death, her condemnation by all the people, the abhorrence of her husband and relations, the tears of her servants, the grief of all her household—she foresaw all this, and yet nothing could shake her fortitude.[22]

Even though she appears to be in a defenseless position, naked in her bath before two lewd luminaries, she acts decisively. She screams. The elders are left without recourse except to react. She has maintained her integrity by going on the offense. All three of Susanna's orations are uttered as soliloquies rather than as dialogue. She speaks to her God and to herself—not to the people around her—and she does not expect to be answered. She wants to express to herself the inward state of her heart. Her soliloquies take on the form of prayers to the all-seeing God who knows her soul and who "knowest the secrets, and knowest all things before they be" (42).[23]

Women as heroines in Jewish culture are rare. Susanna's heroism is unique. Unlike the assertive Jael, who drives a tent peg through the temple of the sleeping Sisera, or the provocative Judith, who beguiles the brutal Holofernes in order to take his head from him, or the prescient Deborah, who leads her people into war, Susanna is a heroine within the strictures of her contemporary culture. She does not attempt to subvert her traditional roles as wife and daughter, but she emerges as a moral hero. She is not intimidated by the "respected" paragons of her society, nor does she succumb to their appeals or even their threats. She is so firm in her refusal of their proposal that it does not occur to them to try to overcome her physically. She is a fascinating mix of shyness and inner strength. Her profound depth of soul naturally attracts us to her, not just because she is a beautiful woman, but because of her dignity, courage, and grace. Her loveliness is more than skin deep.[24]

The moral of this diminutive tale is apparent—one person who stands with the Lord is enough to overcome any odds. In fact, the Lord likes to be the underdog. Consider the instances of Moses against the prowess of Pharaoh; Gideon and his three hundred men against the Midianites, who are as numerous as grasshoppers (Judges 6:3, 5); or Elisha against the king of Syria and his mighty armies (2 Kings 6:15–23). The well-respected elders of the community do not understand or perceive the truth, but a woman who takes reflective walks in her garden and a young boy from out of town do. With God's help, even this woman and this boy can bring about justice and reveal truth.[25]

Notes

1. Steven Walker, *Seven Ways of Looking at Susanna* (Provo: Center for the Study of Christian Values in Literature, Brigham Young University, 1984), 8.

2. T. J. Wray, *Good Girls, Bad Girls: The Enduring Lessons of Twelve Women in the Old Testament* (Lantham: Rowman and Littlefield, 2008), 163–64.

3. Ibid.

4. Ibid., 164.

5. Megan McKenna, *Leave Her Alone* (Maryknoll: Orbis Books, 2000), 72.

6. Leviticus 20:10 reads, "The adulterer and adulteress shall surely be put to death."

7. Wray, *Good Girls, Bad Girls: The Enduring Lessons of Twelve Women in the Old Testament*, 166–67.

8. Ibid., 167

9. Walker, *Seven Ways of Looking at Susanna*, 75.

10. Wray, *Good Girls, Bad Girls: The Enduring Lessons of Twelve Women in the Old Testament*, 167.

11. Walker, *Seven Ways of Looking at Susanna*, 48.

12. Ibid., 49.

13. Ibid., 11.

14. Ibid., 49.

15. Ibid., 83–85.

16. R. A. F. MacKenzie, "The Meaning of the Susanna Story," *Canadian Journal of Theology*, vol. 3, no. 4. Oct. 1957, 213; see also Walker, *Seven Ways of Looking at Susanna*, 94–95.

17. C. J. Ball, "Additions to Daniel: II. The History of Susanna," *The Holy Bible According to the Authorized Version (A.D. 1611)*, 2 vols. Edited by Henry Wace. (London: John Murray, 1888), 2:330.

18. Walker, *Seven Ways of Looking at Susanna*, 13.

19. Ibid., 14–15.

20. Ibid., 16–19.

21. Ibid., 32.

22. Bruce M. Metzger, *An Introduction to the Apocrypha* (New York: Oxford University Press, 1957), 112.

23. Walker, *Seven Ways of Looking at Susanna*, 73.

24. Ibid., 23–25.

25. Ibid., 45.

CHAPTER 3

Judith: Losing Your Head to a Beautiful Girl
The Book of Judith

THE BOOK OF JUDITH IS the story of one woman who successfully brings down the powerful Assyrian military machine. It contrasts the weakness of this woman with the invincible power of the formidable commander-in-chief of the Assyrian forces. It is a story in the tradition of Deborah and Jael, where God delivers the enemy "into the hand of a woman" and she emerges victorious. *The Book of Judith* is one of the fourteen books of the Apocrypha and was probably composed in the second century B.C.[1] Many artists have portrayed Judith's triumph in paintings during the fifteenth and sixteenth centuries, including Michelangelo, who included a scene from Judith's story on the ceiling of the Sistine Chapel.

Judith is a Hebrew name that means "Jewess." This appellation aptly describes the woman who bears it. She is a deeply pious woman, whose faith flows from Israel's covenant with God. She sees Israel's power as stemming from its willingness to be different from all other nations. Judith's piety does not preclude her from being feminine, and she understands the art of tasteful make-up and flattering clothes. It's Judith's loveliness that eventually brings down the Assyrian juggernaut, Holofernes, giving new meaning to the phrase, "if looks could kill."

The first seven chapters of *The Book of Judith* are not just a boring recital of Assyrian military victories. These chapters establish the gargantuan prowess of the Assyrian army and the degree of faith required to challenge and defeat such might. *The Anchor Bible Dictionary* asserts that the first seven chapters serve as an effective and indispensable foil for the last nine chapters. "In the first half, . . ." it states, "Nebuchadnezzar and Holofernes, resorting to fear and brute, masculine force, [win] many battles." They set the stage for the arrival of Judith on the scene in the eighth chapter. In the last half, Judith, with her " 'soft' feminine beauty" and charm, bolstered by her great faith, wins the war.[2]

The story begins when Nebuchadnezzar, the king of Assyria, decides to wage war against the king of the Medes, Arphaxad. Nebuchadnezzar invites his vassal states to join him in the fight, and while many of the states in the east rally to his aid, his subjects in the west, from Cilicia in the north to Ethiopia in the south, scoff at his request for help. Greatly incensed, Nebuchadnezzar swears that someday he will punish them for their insubordination. Finally, after he has destroyed Arphaxad and his "invincible" city, Ecbatana, he turns against the vassals that have rejected his invitation.

Commissioning Holofernes, his greatest general, to exact revenge on those states who have defied him, Nebuchadnezzar tells his plan: those nations who will submit to Holofernes by offering tokens of earth and water will be dealt with later. Those who will not capitulate are to be slaughtered and looted without mercy. In response, Holofernes deploys his massive army of 120,000 soldiers, 12,000 mounted bowmen, and the support personnel needed to maintain a company of that size. Starting from Nineveh, they march to Cilicia (a distance of three hundred miles) in just three days. Then the army wreaks havoc on its way through Put and Lud, plundering their inhabitants on the way. As he proceeds through Mesopotamia, Holofernes' army levels towns and destroys the inhabitants as it goes. Many seacoast towns appeal to his mercy, saying, "Here we servants of Nebuchadnezzar the Great King lie before you. . . . Our cities and their inhabitants are your slaves; come and treat them as you see fit" (*Judith* 3:1, 4).³ Holofernes responds by tearing down their sanctuaries and groves, "in order that all the nations should worship Nebuchadnezzar alone, and that all their tongues and tribes should call upon him as a god" (3:8). So much for freedom of religion.

Holofernes and his army then make their way toward Esdraelon, near Judea, and set up their camp there. The Israelites in Judea, having recently returned from exile and rededicated their beloved temple in Jerusalem, are understandably petrified. They have heard what Holofernes has "done to the heathen, and how he [has] plundered all their temples and destroyed them" (4:1–2). Despite the great destruction in the states around them, Israel decides to hold out. Many cities secure their hilltops and prepare provisions for war. The high priest in Jerusalem orders the cities of Bethulia and Bethomesthaim on the northern boundary to fortify their passes, "since access to Judea and Jerusalem was through a narrow pass wide enough for only two men at a time to pass." The people of Judea, young and old alike, wear sackcloth, and fast and pray for Yahveh's help to protect them and their temple.⁴

The Anchor Bible Dictionary states that when Holofernes hears of this defiance, he is "both surprised and angered. Demanding information on the Israelites, he [gets] a full report from one Achior, leader of the Ammonites. Achior [tells] how the Israelites lived first in Chaldea, next in Mesopotamia, and then in Canaan. There they grew rich until a terrible famine forced them to Egypt, where they were ultimately enslaved by Pharaoh." He describes how their God had interceded on their behalf to free them, even parting the Red Sea for them to make their escape. The Israelites then invaded the land of the Amorites and destroyed all the inhabitants of the land. Achior tells Holofernes, "As long as they [do] not sin against their God, they [prosper]" (5:17). When they turned from their God, he no longer protected them, and they were conquered and carried away captive, their temple destroyed. They have turned once again to their God and returned from their exile. Achior tells the Assyrians that if the Israelites are sinning against God presently, then their God will allow the Assyrians to defeat them, but if not, they cannot be defeated.⁵

Holofernes does not think much of Achior's assessment of the

Israelites' invulnerability. He says, "And who are you, Achior, . . . that you should act the prophet among us as you have done today, and tell us not to make war upon the people of Israel because their God will protect them? What god is there except Nebuchadnezzar? He will put forth his strength and destroy them off the face of the earth, and their god will not save them" (6:2–3). Holofernes decides to let Achior share the fate of the Israelites, and he is seized and deposited at the base of a hill outside Bethulia, one of the Israelite cities. The Israelites discover him, and after hearing his story, they take him home with them.

When the Israelites see the great numbers of the Assyrians encamped against them, they are greatly troubled and say to each other, "These people will lick up the face of the whole country, and neither the high mountains nor the valleys nor the hills will bear their weight" (7:4). They have heard the horror stories about Holofernes and are seized by panic. They fast and pray in a hysteria of fear, donning sackcloth and ashes and begging for God to come and deliver them from Holofernes' immense and brutal army.

Holofernes, after consulting with the leaders of Esau and the Moabites, determines to seize the water sources of the city Bethulia, letting thirst overwhelm the people and force them to surrender their town. After thirty-four days without water, the cisterns of Bethulia start to dry out. The inhabitants plead with their town leaders to surrender, saying, "It is better for us to be plundered by them, for we shall become slaves and our lives will be preserved" (7:27). Then Uzziah, their leader, asks them to take courage and hold out five days longer. He tells them that if God has not sent relief to them after that time, he will surrender the city.

Everyone in the city accepts the compromise except the beautiful Judith, the rich young widow of Manasseh, who is known for her devotion. Since her husband's death three and a half years earlier, she has been in widow's mourning, wearing sackcloth and fasting every day except when it is specifically prohibited. She is described as "very beautiful and fair to see," and has ample resources because her husband "had left her gold and silver, and male and female slaves, and cattle and lands" (8:7). Most important, "There was nobody who spoke ill of her, for she feared God with all her heart" (8:8).

Judith summons the elders of the town to her home and censures them. She scolds them for attempting to put God to the test and giving him a time limit in which to save them. She feels that this testing of the God of Israel is just what their inconstant ancestors did. This lack of faith on the part of the town leaders and the people is tantamount to a betrayal of the covenant. She deals with the elders harshly, accusing them of offense against God. Her words sting them.

Judith explains that God is not like men, who can be threatened or cajoled, but that he does as he pleases. If he wishes to deliver them, he will do so, but they must continue to trust in him because he is the only god they have ever known. She suggests that perhaps God is trying them, as he did Abraham and Isaac, to see how pure their hearts are. She says, "for he has not tried us with fire, as he did them, to search their hearts, and he has not taken vengeance upon us, but the Lord scourges those who come near him, to instruct them" (8:27). Then "Mayor" Uzziah reminds her that they have sworn an oath to the people, which they cannot break, and snidely suggests that she, who has always been wise and righteous, petition God for their deliverance: "For you are a devout woman, and the Lord will send rain to fill our cisterns, and we will not faint any more" (8:31). Judith responds to this with a counterproposal—she and her maid will go out of the gate that evening, and within the allotted five days the Lord will deliver Israel by her hand. But they must not inquire about her plans, for she will not tell them what she is going to do until it is done. The rulers give her their blessing and are gone.

Judith then puts ashes on her head and prays that God will decimate the Assyrian forces threatening Jerusalem and its temple. She cries, "Look at their arrogance, direct your anger upon their heads, put in the hand of a widow like me the strength to do what I have planned. . . . For your strength is not in numbers, nor your might in the strong, but you are the God of the lowly, the helper of the inferior, the champion of the weak, the protector of the neglected, the savior of the despairing" (9:9, 11). She also prays for a beguiling tongue to overcome her enemy. After completing her spiritual preparation, she returns to her house where she prepares for battle. With her maid's help, she bathes and anoints herself with expensive ointment. She dresses herself in her most alluring attire, "and [makes] herself very beautiful to attract the eyes of any men who might see her." She braids her hair, puts on a headdress, and puts on "her anklets and bracelets and rings and earrings and all her ornaments" (10:4). Then, taking a bag of provisions to last her for a few days—an oil jar, flour made from barley, and small cakes made from dried figs and fine flour—she and her maid go out to the gate of the town where the town leaders meet them. After obtaining their blessing, the women bid them farewell and make their way through the valley.

After they have gone a short distance, she and her maid are arrested by an Assyrian patrol. When they ask her who she is and where she is going, she replies, "I am a daughter of the Hebrews, and I am escaping from their presence because they are going to be given to you to devour. I am going to the presence of Holofernes, the commander-in-chief of your army, to give him a true report, and I will show him a way by which he can go and become master of all the hilly country without losing from his men one living body or spirit" (10:12–13). Upon hearing her words, and being charmed by her beauty, they escort her directly to Holofernes' tent. Wondering at her loveliness, they say to one another, "Who can despise [the Israelites], when they have such women among them? For it is not right to leave one man of them alive, for if we let them go they will be able to beguile the whole earth" (10:19). This statement is more accurate than they perceive at that moment.

When Judith enters Holofernes' tent, he assures her that she will not be harmed because she has chosen to serve King Nebuchadnezzar. Judith flatters Holofernes with praise for his military prowess, "wisdom," and "cleverness of mind." She promises, "I will declare nothing false to my lord tonight. If you follow out the words of your maidservant [herself], God will fully carry out the matter with you, and my lord will not fall short of his designs" (11:5–6). Judith's carefully worded promise drips with irony. Holofernes is completely oblivious to the sarcasm, but it is not lost on the reader. He thinks "my lord" means himself, but Judith's lord is none other than the God of Israel.

Judith next addresses the topic of Achior's words to the Assyrian council about the invincibility of Israel under God's protection. She expresses her concurrence with Achior's assessment, that "our nation cannot be punished, the sword cannot prevail against them, unless they sin against their God" (11:10). However, she says Israel is on the verge of doing exactly that. Because of the siege against the city, the citizens of Bethulia will soon be forced to eat things forbidden by God—food consecrated to the Lord and his priests. She tells him that she will go out every evening to pray, and, because she is devout, God will reveal to her when this profanation occurs. When this happens, she will personally guide Holofernes and his army to Jerusalem, where he will set up his throne. She tells him that this foreknowledge has been revealed to her, and that she has been sent to him. She has set the trap and needs but wait until he takes the bait.

Holofernes is greatly pleased by her intelligence and, being charmed by her beauty, he believes all her words. He invites her to join him for dinner, but she declines, saying that she cannot eat his food "for it might give offense" (12:2). When she says that she will eat her own food (food acceptable under the Mosaic law), Holofernes asks where he might obtain new supplies for her when her own run out. To this she asserts, "As surely as you are alive, my lord, your slave will not use up the things I have with me before the Lord carries out by my hand the things he has resolved upon" (12:4). Again, Judith utters a statement whose true message is lost upon Holofernes.

For the next three days, Judith stays in her own tent, leaving the Assyrian camp only at night to wash in the spring and pray. Afterward, she stays in her tent until she has her food in the evening. On the fourth day, aspiring to ravish her, Holofernes invites Judith to a small dinner party he is having in his tent. She accepts, saying, "And who am I, to refuse my lord? For I will make haste to do everything that is pleasing in his sight, and this will be my boast to the day of my death" (12:14). Again, what Judith hopes to boast about is very different from what Holofernes believes she hopes. "My lord" in Greek is *ho kyrios mou*. The general assumes Judith is addressing him, but every Greek-speaking Jew reading the account would have understood the Greek translation of Yahveh in her words.[6]

"Dressed to kill" in her most elaborate finery, Judith enters Holofernes' presence and reclines before him at the table. (Reclining on pillows around the table was the accepted eating posture at that time.) Holofernes' "mind was amazed and his heart was stirred, and he was exceedingly desirous of intimacy with her, for he had been watching for an opportunity to deceive her ever since he had seen her" (12:16). She then takes what her slave has prepared and eats and drinks before Holofernes. He, being delighted with her, drinks "a very great deal of wine, more than he had ever drunk on one day since he was born" (12:20). By the time everyone else has discreetly withdrawn for the night, Holofernes is lying prostrate on his bed, dead drunk. Judith sends her servant to the door to act as a lookout. Judith stands beside Holofernes' bed and says in her heart, "Lord, God of all power, look favorably at this hour upon the works of my hands for the exaltation of Jerusalem" (13:4–5). She grabs Holofernes by the hair of the head, and, praying for strength, she strikes him on the neck twice with his own sword with all her might, severing his head from his body. She then rolls his body onto the floor and pulls the canopy down from the bed pillars. After a little while, she goes out to get her maid and has her drop the decapitated head into their food sack. Then, as is their nightly custom, the two of them go out to the ravine "to pray." They pass through the camp and go up the mountain to the gates of Bethulia.

Judith calls out to the watchmen to open the gate and call the elders of the town together. When they are assembled, she says to them in a loud voice, "Praise God who has not withdrawn his mercy from the house of Israel, but has shattered our enemies by my hand this very night!" (13:14). She takes the head out of the bag as proof she speaks truly and assures them that her virtue is untarnished. Then she plots out the tactics they must employ the next day. She tells them to behave as if they are coming down to fight the Assyrians, but they must delay. When the Assyrians go to awaken their general, they will find him headless and be thrown into a panic, because they too are "headless." They will flee before the Israelites, who can then pursue and destroy them.

Judith has Achior brought before her so that he might behold the man who had struck such fear into him and turned him over to the Israelites as though to his death. When he views Holofernes' severed head, he collapses to the ground. When he revives, he falls at Judith's feet and begs her to tell him all that she has done. After listening to her amazing tale, Achior believes in the God of Israel, accepts circumcision, and becomes a Jew.

When dawn comes, the Bethulians hang the head of Holofernes from the wall and prepare for battle. The Assyrians, seeing their preparations, hurry to wake up their general and fall into a frenzy when they see what has befallen him. Uzziah, the leader of Bethulia, sends messengers to all the Israelite cites in the region, and they join the Bethulians in attacking the Assyrians, pursuing them as far as Damascus. The remaining inhabitants of Bethulia come and pillage the camp of the Assyrians and become very rich. In fact, it takes thirty days to plunder the camp. Judith is given the tent of Holofernes and all of his silver dishes, beds, and furniture. When the other Israelites return after the slaughter of the Assyrian army, they take what remains and get "a great quantity of spoil, for there was a very great amount of it" (15:7).

The high priest Joakim and the Jewish Council come down to witness the scene and to pay their respects to Judith. They extol her, saying, "You are the exaltation of Jerusalem, you are the great glory of Israel, you are the great boast of our nation. You have done all this with your hand; you have done Israel good, and God is pleased with it" (15:10). All the women of Israel also come to see her and dance in her honor. She responds in kind, leading the women in a victory dance as they journey to Jerusalem. Judith gives them olive branches to braid wreathes, and they come into the city singing. The men of Israel follow them, wearing their armor and garlands, singing as they go. Along the way, Judith sings a song of praise to the Lord, telling of the proud Assyrians' boast to burn up the borders of Israel, to kill her young men, to throw her babies on the ground, to take her children as spoils, and to have her young girls as plunder. She exalts, "The Lord Almighty brought them to nought By the hand of a woman," and "Her sandal ravished his eye, And her beauty captivated his soul. The scimitar passed through his neck" (16:6, 9). In the second part of the song, the focus shifts to God, who is wonderfully strong and merciful to those who fear him. Sacrifices and burnt offerings performed by a person are insignificant to the Lord in comparison to the worshipful state of a person's heart toward him.

Once all of the people arrive in Jerusalem, they worship God and offer him their heartfelt sacrifices. Judith dedicates to God all of Holofernes' dishes that she has received, as well as the rich canopy she had taken from over his bed. The Israelites remain in Jerusalem for three months, celebrating continuously. When Judith finally returns home, she continues to live on her estate and remains true to the memory of her deceased husband. Although many men desire to marry her, she does not remarry. Before she dies at the ripe old age of a hundred and five, she frees her devoted maid and divides her property among her relatives. For as long as she lives and for a long time after she dies, no one dares terrorize the Israelites.

For many centuries, scholars have questioned *The Book of Judith*'s historical validity because of its carelessness with well-known historical and geographical facts. Chief among these historical errors is the glaring statement that Nebuchadnezzar was the king of the Assyrians, because as most students of the Bible know, Nebuchadnezzar was the king of Babylonia, *not* Assyria. Its most blatant geographical error is the assertion that Holofernes' huge army completed its 300-mile trek from Nineveh to Cilicia in only *three* days. Also, the details of his maneuvers through Africa and Asia Minor are filled with conspicuous errors.

Various theories have been proposed to explain these problems. Perhaps a failure to recognize *The Book of Judith* as a quintessentially ironic book is responsible for the large number of misinterpretations regarding it. The author uses irony so lavishly that readers often do not realize that he means the opposite of what he says. The first verse in the first chapter of *The Book of Judith* is a good example. "In the twelfth year of the reign of Nebuchadnezzar, who ruled over the Assyrians in the great city of Nineveh." One modern scholar, Charles Cutler Torrey, maintains that *The Book of Judith*'s ancient audience would have understood this verse as ironic, even as a modern reader would understand the irony in a story which began, "It happened at the time when Napoleon Bonaparte was king of England, and Otto von Bismark was on the throne of Mexico."[7] Such an understanding would have been tantamount to the storyteller giving his listeners a "solemn wink" as he delivered this opening sentence.[8]

This interpretation would remove *The Book of Judith* from being a historical record and transfer it into the "Everyman" category. Instead of pitting Nebuchadnezzar and Holofernes against Judith and the Israelites, it becomes instead a contest between Yahveh and any pagan philosophy or force that opposes him. While seeming to recount one concrete encounter between a pagan king and Israel, the author is "actually speaking of an encounter which transcends history and becomes the model of opposition to any and every pagan ruler...

Thus, the author invokes the pattern of the Exodus. . . . the contest in Egypt is really one between Pharaoh and Yahveh."[9] Interesting as this representation might be, however, such departure from historical facts no doubt caused this heroic story to be excluded from the Jewish canon.

Judith is clearly an ironic figure. *The Anchor Bible Dictionary* explains that while Judith is a beautiful and alluring widow, she lives in a state of celibacy after her husband's death. Although childless, she gives spiritual and political rebirth to her nation. In spite of being wealthy, she spends most of her life fasting. Notwithstanding her feminine appearance, she ruthlessly cuts off the head of Holofernes with her own hands.[10]

Holofernes is also a portrait of irony. "Able to conquer the entire west, he [is] unable to conquer Bethulia; intending to master Judith, he was mastered by her—by the very sword . . . he himself had used to claim the lives of so many others."[11] He loses his head to a beautiful girl indeed!

Even the minor characters in the story exhibit irony. Achior, who is an experienced warrior, faints when he sees the head of Holofernes. Although he is a pagan he also shows "more faith in Israel's God than [does] the Israelite magistrate of Bethulia, Uzziah, who in 'womanly' fashion" hides "behind the safety of high walls while Judith, in 'manly' fashion," goes out to meet the enemy. The Assyrian soldiers who apprehend Judith and her maid end up escorting her to Holofernes' tent, a prime example of "the captive taking captive the captors."[12]

Judith exhibits many of the characteristics of notable biblical heroines. Like Jael in the book of Judges, she kills a general with his own sword and receives the accolades of her people for her act of courage and deliverance. Like Deborah and Miriam, she sings her song of victory.

Although some have disparaged Judith's actions in relation to Holofernes—her shameless flattery, her carefully-worded phrases meant to deceive, and her brutal assassination—judged by the standards of her own society, Judith *is* deeply religious. She is devoutly pious, she remains true to the memory of her husband and never remarries, she prays constantly (fasting as often as is allowed), and adheres strictly to the Jewish dietary laws. She is totally dedicated to her God and fiercely patriotic to her country, trusting in God to rescue his people despite extremely difficult circumstances. Considering the patriarchal society in which she lives, she is a prime example of God's ability to defeat any enemy—no matter how invincible—by the hand of a "weak" woman.

The story of Judith is "clearly a rescue story in which the female plays the heroine and saves the male (Israel) from the hand of Holofernes."[13] It is in the tradition of Jael and Deborah, where the heroines enter the story at a late point in the plot and act quickly and decisively as the stories move rapidly toward their climaxes. Both Judith and Jael are marginal members of Israelite society—Judith as a widow, and Jael as a member of a non-Israelite clan. "This fact emphasizes the theme in both stories of the weak (symbolized by the female) triumphing over the strong (symbolized by the male) with the help of Yahveh. . . . Deborah and Judith are both secure that their convictions are in accordance with God's will."[14] According to the additional insights offered by the pseudepigrapha, Jael also shares this certainty, because she asks for and receives a sign that what she is about to do is according to God's will. Just as Deborah gives Barak his "marching orders," in the book of Judges, so Judith gives the elders of Bethulia the battle strategy they are to employ after Holofernes' death is discovered. In each of these stories, Yahveh will triumph by the hand of a woman. Both Jael and Judith take weapons in their hands to annihilate generals. Both assassins are successful because their victims are asleep, one from strong drink, one from goat's milk, a well-known soporific. The deaths of Deborah and Judith are followed by periods of peace; no enemy dares encroach upon the land for forty years.[15]

Judith is a classic example of an *ezer*. She is strong. She is a rescuer. Her example inspires women in any age to use creativity, shrewdness, faith, and courage to accomplish seemingly impossible feats.

Notes

1. *The Anchor Bible Dictionary*, vol. 3. Edited by David Noel Freedman (New York: Doubleday, 1992), 1123; see also Megan McKenna, *Leave Her Alone* (Maryknoll, New York: Orbis Books, 2000), 183.

2. Ibid., 1120.

3. Edgar J. Goodspeed, "The Book of Judith," in *The Apocrypha: An American*

Translation. (New York: Vintage Books, 1989), 137. All references from the Book of Judith will be taken from this source.

4. *The Anchor Bible Dictionary,* 1118.

5. Ibid.

6. Sidnie Ann White, "In the Steps of Jael and Deborah: Judith as Heroine" in *"No One Spoke Ill of Her": Essays on Judith.* Edited by James C. VanderKam. (Atlanta: Scholars Press, 1992), 8.

7. C. C Torrey, *The Apocryphal Literature: A Brief Introduction* (New Haven: 1945), 89.

8. The storyteller takes great pains to tell his audience that they are listening to a good story, not an account of actual historical events. This attempt at humor and irony is apparently lost on most modern commentators, who think the author of the narrative is attempting to give an accurate portrayal of a real historical setting and are amazed at his ignorance.

9. John Craghan, "Introduction to the Book of Judith," in *The Old Testament Message: A Biblical-Theological Commentary, vol. 16, Esther, Judith, Tobit, Jonah, Ruth* (Wilmington: Michael Glazier, 1982), 70.

10. *The Anchor Bible Dictionary,* 1121.

11. Ibid.

12. Ibid.

13. Craghan, "Introduction to the Book of Judith," 71.

14. White, "In the Steps of Jael and Deborah: Judith as Heroine," 6–7.

15. Ibid., 8–12.

CHAPTER 4

Aseneth: Wife of Joseph and Paragon of Proselytes
Joseph and Aseneth, Genesis 41:45, 50; 46:20

THE OLD TESTAMENT RECORDS THAT Pharaoh gave Joseph Aseneth,[1] the daughter of Potiphera, Priest of On, for his wife (Genesis 41:45). No further information is provided about Aseneth except that her name is chronicled as being the wife of Joseph in Genesis 41:45, 50; and in 46:20. She is also listed as Joseph's wife in the pseudepigraphical books of *Demetrius the Chronographer* (Fragment 2:12), *Jubilees* (34:20, 44:24), and the *Testament of Joseph* (20:3), but no additional details are furnished. Jewish legend quickly filled in the details surrounding the intriguing mystery of Aseneth. The longest of these stories is in the book of *Joseph and Aseneth*, written by an anonymous author between the first century B.C. and the second century A.D.

Joseph, a prominent figure in Jewish literature, is portrayed as an exemplar of righteousness in both Genesis and the *Testament of the Twelve Patriarchs*. His marriage to the daughter of the high priest of Heliopolis was bound to create theological problems for Orthodox

Judaism. The pseudepigraphical book of *Joseph and Aseneth* deals with this problem, describing Aseneth's repentance and conversion from idolatry and portraying her as the archetypal proselyte. Other Jewish sources propose alternate resolutions to the Aseneth-as-pagan dilemma.[2]

Aseneth is portrayed as being a virgin of eighteen years, very tall and beautiful, "beyond all virgins on the earth." The narrative especially notes that she had "nothing similar to the virgins of the Egyptians, but she was in every respect similar to the daughters of the Hebrews; and she was tall as Sarah and handsome as Rebecca and beautiful as Rachel" (*Joseph and Aseneth* 1:5). Though no paparazzi were around to tout her handsomeness, the fame of her beauty spreads throughout the land and many noblemen and princes, including the son of Pharaoh, seek her hand in marriage. This description is almost identical to that of Psyche in the story by Apuleius: "The fame of her surpassing beauty spread over the earth, and everywhere men journeyed to gaze upon her with wonder and adoration and to do her homage as though she were in truth one of the immortals."[3] I guess you could say that she was one of the earliest supermodels.

To all these entreaties, Aseneth remains scornful, and she is "boastful and arrogant with everyone" (2:1). She is depicted as living in a splendid tower above her father's palace, unseen by men, where she worships the gods of the Egyptians daily.

One day, as Joseph comes into the land of Heliopolis to gather the surplus grain of the region, he sends a message to Pentephres, Aseneth's father, announcing that he will be dining with him that evening. Aseneth dresses herself to meet her parents, putting on jewels that have the pictures and names of idols engraved upon them. As she dutifully greets her parents, her father gives laudatory praise of Joseph and proposes to hand her over to him to be his wife. (It is interesting to note that it is Aseneth's father who proposes to give her to Joseph to wife, in contrast to the Genesis account where Pharaoh gives her to Joseph.) When Aseneth hears this proposition, *Joseph and Aseneth* records that beads of "red sweat" pour over her face and she becomes "furious with great anger" (4:9). She daringly responds, "Why does my lord and my father speak words such as these, to hand me over, like a captive, to a man (who is) an alien, and a fugitive, and (was) sold (as a slave)?" (4:9).

She reiterates the facts that he is a "shepherd's son," an occupation despised by the Egyptians, was caught in the act when sleeping with his mistress, and is an interpreter of dreams like the "older women of the Egyptians." Utterly refusing his proposition, she announces that she will be married to the king's firstborn son. So much for the idea of an arranged marriage.

At that moment, Joseph's arrival is announced, and Aseneth rushes out of the presence of her parents, retreating to her chambers to watch the arrival of Joseph through the window of her tower. He is adorned in exquisite finery, with the royal staff in his left hand and an olive branch in his right. As he enters the court, Pentephres and his wife and the entire family prostrate themselves on the ground before him.

Aseneth has a very strong reaction to the sight of Joseph. He is "easy on the eyes." The story continues, "And Aseneth saw Joseph on his chariot and was strongly cut (to the heart), and her soul was crushed, and her knees were paralyzed, and her entire body trembled, and she was filled with great fear" (6:1). She marvels that she could have once disdained one who she now refers to as "the sun from heaven" and a "son of God." In using such language to describe Joseph, Aseneth calls to the mind of the reader the fact that Pharaoh is viewed as the son of the sun god, Re, and would be described in like terms. George W. E. Nickelsburg writes that this symbolizes Aseneth's twofold conversion. "By describing Joseph in language appropriate to Pharaoh's son, she is not only making a marital choice," but is emphasizing her conversion "from the gods of Egypt to the God of Joseph."[4] She wonders where she might flee and hide from his face since she has spoken wickedly of him. She presumes that one filled with such light must be able to perceive all that is hidden. She utters a prayer to the "Lord, God of Joseph," that she might be Joseph's maidservant and slave forever. With one glance, Aseneth abandons her former gods in favor of the God of Joseph, and exchanges her disdain for a would-be suitor for a pledge of eternal loyalty as his lowly slave.

After Joseph enters Pentephres's house, his feet are washed and a separate table is set up before him because he considers eating with the Egyptians an abomination. As he looks up, he sees Aseneth leaning through her window and he immediately asks her father to have her leave the house at once. Joseph's reaction to Aseneth is, like hers, one of fear, but for a much different reason. Apparently, his beauty has inflamed the women he has had contact with, and he is afraid that this one might molest him as well.[5] He had despised them all and refused their overtures. He was determined not to sin before the Lord, "nor in the face of [his] father Jacob," who advised him against "associating with a strange woman" (7:4–5). When Pentephres informs him that this woman is no stranger, but their daughter and like a sister to him, and "a virgin hating every man" (7:8), his fear vanishes and he professes that he will love her from that day as his sister.

When Aseneth's mother fetches Aseneth and presents her to Joseph, her father bids her to kiss her "brother." As she is about to comply with his request, Joseph prevents her by stretching forth his right hand and putting it "on her chest between her two breasts"[6] (8:5). He says that it is not fit for a man who worships God with his mouth to kiss the mouth of one who "will bless with her mouth dead and dumb idols and eat from their table bread of strangulation and drink from their libation a cup of insidiousness and anoint herself with ointment of destruction" (8:5–6). This strong statement reflects Joseph's feelings, but is not what we would call polite. He affirms that it is fitting that he kiss only his mother, his sisters, and the wife of his bed; to kiss any others would be an "abomination before the Lord God" (8:7). Upon hearing Joseph's words, Aseneth is again "cut (to the heart)" (8:8) and distressed and, although she keeps staring at Joseph, her eyes fill with tears. Besides being cut off from "the living God" because of her worship of deaf and dumb idols, her defilement has imperiled her relationship with Joseph.

Joseph, being sensitive and perceptive, is himself "cut (to the heart)" (8:9), and he places his hand on her head and blesses her. He asks the Lord to "bless this virgin, and renew her by [his] spirit" (8:9). He prays that God will "number her among [his] people that [he has] chosen before all (things) came into being" (8:9) and that she might one day "enter [God's] rest" (8:9) and "live in . . . eternal life for ever (and) ever" (8:9). Joseph departs, after announcing that he will return a week later. After Joseph's departure, Aseneth rejoices because of Joseph's blessing, but she is filled with much distress and weeps with "great and bitter weeping" (9:1) and repents of her worship of her former gods and idols.

Aseneth withdraws to her tower where she repents, prays, and fasts for days. She exchanges her royal robes for sackcloth and throws her idols and their rich sacrificial food out the window. She flings the food to strange dogs because, she says to herself, "By no means must my dogs eat from my dinner and from the sacrifice of the idols" (10:13). After scattering ashes over her floor, she strikes her breast often and cries bitterly, falling upon her ashes and weeping "with great and bitter weeping all night with sighing and screaming until daybreak" (10:15). When Aseneth rises at daybreak, she sees that there is "much mud from her tears and from the ashes" (10:16). In this manner, Aseneth passes the next seven days.

On the eighth day, Aseneth lifts her head just a little from the floor and the ashes on which she is lying, it being impossible to control her limbs because of the want of food for seven days. She continues sighing and weeping and sprinkling ashes on her head, and, without opening her mouth, she utters a pitiful prayer to the true God of Joseph. She does not vocalize her prayer because she feels her mouth is defiled and unworthy of addressing God.[7] She acknowledges that she is hated by her parents for destroying their gods and hated by Joseph's God for worshiping strange idols. (Sometimes, you just can't please anyone.) She declares that she has heard that the Hebrew God is compassionate and long-suffering, and she hopes he will have mercy on her and protect her, because she feels she is now an orphan.

After this invocation, Aseneth again prays in her heart without opening her mouth, pleading for courage to ask God for forgiveness. Spreading her hand eastward and looking towards heaven, Aseneth finally opens her mouth to God, confessing her sins and praying for acceptance. After acknowledging his great power and omnipotence, she confesses her former pride and sin in worshiping dead and dumb idols, which she avows was done "in ignorance" (12:5). She pleads for God to rescue her and to snatch her away as a "child-loving father" (12:8) from the "wild old lion" (12:9)—a metaphor for the devil, who is persecuting her as a new convert "because he is the father of the gods of the Egyptians" (12:9) whom she has abandoned. She entreats God to note her acts of repentance in forsaking all her former opulence, her raiment, her inheritance, and her blasphemy against the "all-beautiful Joseph" (13:14). She confesses that she loves him beyond her own soul and only yearns to be his servant forever.

After Aseneth's confession to the Lord, she sees the morning star rise in the east and takes it as a sign of her acceptance. As she continues to look, "great and unutterable light" (14:3) appears and a man comes from heaven and stands at her head in her chamber. She marvels that he has come because the tower is high and the door of her chamber is bolted. The glorious, shining man informs her that he is the commander of the whole host of the Most High, and that he has a message for her. He instructs her to go to her second chamber and change out of her mourning attire and put on a clean linen robe and the girdle of her virginity before he conveys the message. She complies with his wishes, adding a linen veil to cover her head.

When Aseneth returns to his presence, the angel bids her remove the veil and take courage because he has heard her confession and has seen her humiliation during the last seven days. He informs her that her name is "written in the book of the living in heaven" (15:4) by his own finger and will not be erased. He tells her that he has given her Joseph for a bridegroom forever and gives her a new name, "City of Refuge" (15:7), because under her wings many people trusting in the Lord God will be sheltered. He tells her that Repentance, the beautiful laughing virgin, is constantly beseeching God on her behalf at all times. The angel then says, "And now listen to me, Aseneth, chaste virgin, and dress in your wedding robe, the ancient and first robe which is laid up in your chamber since eternity, and put around you all your wedding ornaments, and adorn yourself as a good bride, and go meet Joseph. For behold, he himself is coming to you today, and he will see you and rejoice" (15:10). A most interesting courtship.

Aseneth rejoices at these words and prostrates herself before this messenger. When she tries to ascertain his name that she might praise him forever, he refuses, saying that "all names written in the book of the Most High are unspeakable" (15:12).

The angel commands Aseneth to bring a honeycomb, which mysteriously appears in her storehouse. Placing his hands upon her head, he transmits to her "the ineffable mysteries of the Most High" (16:14) and bids her eat of the honeycomb, which is the spirit of life, made by the bees of paradise from the roses of life. She tells him she realizes that this honeycomb has proceeded from his mouth, and he smiles at her understanding. He breaks off a portion of the comb for her, assuring her that she has now eaten "bread of life, and drunk a cup of immortality, and been anointed with ointment of incorruptibility"[8] (16:16). He promises that her "flesh (will) flourish like flowers of life from the ground of the Most High, and [her] bones will grow strong like the cedars of the paradise of delight of God," and that her "youth will not see old age, and [her] beauty will not fail for ever" (16:16).

The heavenly man marks the comb with a cross and makes white bees arise from it. They encircle Aseneth, and form another comb on her mouth. Aseneth beseeches the man to bless her seven virgins, and he complies with her request. She sees the heavenly man disappear in a chariot of fire with horses of lightning, and she is amazed that she has spoken boldly to such a noble and glorious messenger. Through her experiences with the angel, Aseneth passes from the agonies of death to the joys of eternal life. In receiving the "ineffable mysteries of the Most High" (16:14), the "lawlessness and irreverence" (12:4) of her idolatry are wiped away, and she is free to partake of the food and drink of immortality.

While Aseneth is still pondering these marvelous events, a messenger arrives announcing Joseph's visit that very day. She calls the steward and commands that a dinner be prepared in Joseph's honor, and the steward of her father's house departs to prepare the house, although he is distressed at the sight of her pitiful condition. Remembering the commandments of the man from heaven, she dresses in her wedding finery and prepares to wash her face. When Aseneth sees herself in the water, she is astonished at the heavenly beauty she sees and does not dare to wash her face for fear the great beauty will wash off. Aseneth is born beautiful and then has even more beauty added—some girls have all the luck! In assuming bridal apparel, Aseneth's appearance is transfigured as a result of the eternal life that is now hers.

When Joseph arrives, Aseneth meets him in the court. He is amazed at her great beauty and, not recognizing her, asks her who she is. Answering, she relates to him the events of the preceding night and the experience with the heavenly messenger. Joseph blesses her and acknowledges the visit of the same messenger. He replies, "And now, come to me, chaste virgin, and why do you stand far away from me?" (19:9). Stretching out his hands to her, he calls Aseneth with "a wink of his eyes" (19:10). Aseneth also stretches out her hands, and, embracing, they kiss each other "for a long time and both [come] to life in their spirit" (19:10). The narrative records that with the first kiss, Joseph gave Aseneth "the spirit of life;" with the second, he gave her "the spirit of wisdom;" and with the third, he gave her "the spirit of truth" (19:11). Who ever imagined there could be such meaning in a kiss? Following this romantic episode, Aseneth leads Joseph into her father's house and brings water to wash his feet. When he protests that a servant should do so, Aseneth replies that she is his maidservant and that "your feet are my feet, and your hands my hands, and your soul my soul, and your feet another (woman) will never wash" (20:4).

When her parents return, they are amazed at the sight of their radiant daughter sitting with Joseph, and they rejoice and give glory to God. Joseph tells them that on the morrow he will visit Pharaoh, who is like a father to him, and Pharaoh will give him Aseneth to wife. That night he stays with Pentephres, but he does not sleep with Aseneth for he says, "It does not befit a man who worships God to sleep with his wife before the wedding" (21:1)—a concept the modern and "enlightened" world has somehow lost.

The next day, Joseph visits Pharaoh at daybreak and asks for Aseneth to be his wife. Pharaoh rejoices and replies, "Behold, is not this one betrothed to you since eternity?" (21:3). Calling Pentephres, who brings his daughter with him before Pharaoh, he too marvels at Aseneth's beauty. Placing his hands on the heads of Joseph and Aseneth, he pronounces a blessing: "May the Lord God the Most High bless you and multiply you and magnify and glorify you forever" (20:6). Afterward, he turns them around face-to-face and joins them by the lips. Following this ceremony, Pharaoh gives a wonderful marriage feast and proclaims that no man should work during the week of Joseph and Aseneth's wedding or he should "surely die" (21:8). A week-long celebration—a wedding planner's dream.

The next section of *Joseph and Aseneth* records Aseneth's psalm in which she confesses her shortcomings to the Lord and gives thanks for all the things she has received, the foremost of which is Joseph, "the Powerful One of God." She expresses her sentiments with these words:

> He pulled me down from my dominating position
> and made me humble after my arrogance,

> and by his beauty he caught me,
> and by his wisdom he grasped me like a fish on a hook,
> and by his spirit, as by bait of life, he ensnared me,
> and by his power confirmed me,
> and brought me to the God of the ages
> and to the chief of the house of the Most High,
> and gave me to eat bread of life,
> and to drink a cup of wisdom,
> and I became his bride for ever and ever. (21:21)

The record continues with the recounting of the years of famine and Jacob's sojourn in the land of Goshen during the second year of the famine. Chapter 22 is an interlude where Joseph and Aseneth decide to visit Jacob. Aseneth is amazed at Jacob's great "beauty" even in his old age. He has snowy white hair, and "the hairs of his head [are] all exceeding close and thick like (those) of an Ethiopian." He has a beard reaching to his chest, and "his old age [is] like the youth of a handsome (young) man," and "his eyes [are] flashing and darting (flashes of) lightning" (22:7). Jacob calls Aseneth and blesses her, and she hangs "on her father's neck like someone hangs onto his father's neck when he returns from fighting into his house" (22:7), and she kisses him. With this kiss, Aseneth's position in the eyes of Israel is validated.

Simeon and Levi escort Joseph and Aseneth home, but Zilpah's and Bilhah's sons are jealous of them and hostile towards them. Aseneth favors Levi because "he [is] a prophet of the Lord and a prudent man, and used to see letters written in heaven by the finger of God" (22:12). He knows the unspeakable mysteries of God and reveals them to Aseneth in secret. Levi is quoted as desiring Aseneth's "place of rest in the highest, . . . and her foundations founded upon a rock of the seventh heaven" (22:13).[9] This episode provides the transition to the last part of the story.

Warning! What follows in this section is a convoluted plot by a jilted lover to win back the girl of his dreams. There is a good chance that the reader may become lost.

Pharaoh's son reappears as Joseph's rival, madly in love with Aseneth and believing that she has been betrothed to him "from the beginning." He seeks the help of Simeon and Levi in murdering Joseph, but his efforts are in vain. While Simeon would have drawn his sword against Pharaoh's son, Levi meekly and cheerfully explains that they are men who worship God and could never harm anyone, especially their own brother. However, he adds, if he insists on this deed, they will unsheathe their swords before him. Drawing their swords, they declare to Pharaoh's son that these are the swords that devastated the Shechemites. Pharaoh's son, seeing the swords flash forth like flames of fire, falls on his face before them in fear.

When the servants of Pharaoh's son inform him that the sons of Zilpah and Bilhah are jealous of Joseph and Aseneth, he plots again and sends for Dan, Gad, Naphtali, and Asher. Lying to them, he fabricates a story about Joseph's intent to kill them and their offspring at their father's death to avoid sharing the inheritance with them. He says he overheard Joseph telling his father, Pharaoh, this plan. Naturally, the brothers are troubled at this news and ask Pharaoh's son for assistance. Pharaoh's son discloses his plot. He promises to kill his father (who is like a father to Joseph), while the brothers ambush Aseneth's carriage in the wadi and kill Joseph while he is distressed over Aseneth's leaving for her vineyard. He promises to give each brother five hundred men, and they agree to join together in the endeavor.

Pharaoh's son, however, fails to kill his father but goes to the wadi with his fifty bowmen, as directed by Dan and Gad. Naphtali and Asher are stricken with remorse and attempt to restrain Dan and Gad with their words but are unsuccessful. Aseneth leaves Joseph's presence and, with her six hundred men, goes on her way to her vineyard through the wadi.

The men ambush Aseneth, and her forerunners are all killed, but she escapes in her carriage with Benjamin sitting at her side. Levi, being a prophet, perceives Aseneth's danger and makes the situation known to his brothers, who immediately arm themselves and follow her. Aseneth is met by Pharaoh's son, and, being afraid, she calls on the name of God. Benjamin hurls a stone at Pharaoh's son and wounds him and continues to kill all of his men with stones from the wadi. Levi and his five brothers pursue the ambushing men, and the six of them kill two thousand men. Dan, Gad, Naphtali, and Asher flee from before their brothers and attempt to kill Aseneth and Benjamin, but Aseneth prays in the face of their drawn swords, and the swords are reduced to ashes. In the face of such a miracle, the wicked brothers prostrate themselves before Aseneth and beg for mercy. They appeal to her to intercede on their behalf before Levi and his brothers. When the sons of Leah appear, Aseneth appeases them and asks them not to return evil for evil upon them because the Lord has protected her from them and melted their swords. Levi perceives their presence in the thicket of reeds but does not declare it to his brothers because of their intense wrath.

Meanwhile, Benjamin attempts to slay the wounded son of Pharaoh with his own sword, but Levi stops him. Levi reiterates Aseneth's argument that men of God do not return evil for evil upon the heads of their enemies. He binds up the wounds of Pharaoh's son and returns him to his father. Three days later, however, the son of Pharaoh dies from his wounds, and the grief suffered by his father precipitates Pharaoh's own death at the age of one hundred and nine. He leaves his kingdom to Joseph, who rules for forty-eight years. After this, Joseph gives the kingdom back to Pharaoh's younger son, who was a baby when Pharaoh died.

The narrative describing the escapades of Pharaoh's son and Joseph's brothers is steeped in betrayal and subterfuge that is very difficult to follow. (Remember, you were forewarned of this fact.) I think the whole point of all of the drama is that Aseneth, a new convert to true worship, is protected by divine and even mystical power. These events have a *Lord of the Rings* flavor to them. The way the story is related, we cannot doubt that God wants Aseneth in his covenant family regardless of what may have actually taken place. These episodes are employed as a second act to the main drama of the story, and they drive home the miraculous nature of events that surround Aseneth's conversion experience. The author of *Joseph and Aseneth* wants to leave no doubt as to Aseneth's worthiness to hold matriarchal status. Like David, she is "a [wo]man after God's own heart" (Acts 13:22).

The pseudepigraphical book *Joseph and Aseneth* reveals several diverse concepts and messages. Certainly, the foremost purpose served by this narrative is the removal of the stumbling block of Aseneth, a non-Jew, marrying a noted Hebrew patriarch. The narrative so strikingly portrays Aseneth as a penitent convert, whose pious tears combine with the ashes on her floor to make mud, that no reader can help but be convinced of the power of her conversion. The beautiful language of her psalm and her prayers only serves to reinforce the sincerity of her total conversion from idolatry and her worthiness to be associated with the splendid Joseph. In describing Aseneth's conversion, the impediment to her marriage to Joseph is removed, and she can be accepted as a matriarch.

In this myth, both Joseph and Aseneth are painted as larger-than-life figures. Pseudepigraphical scholar C. Burchard points out that in this work, like in Greek romance, the author uses motifs that stem from mythical and astrological contexts (1:4–6, 14:1–3). Joseph reigns after Pharaoh's death for forty-eight years even though, realistically, he could have turned the rule over to Pharaoh's son decades earlier.

Aseneth's initial pride and boldness are soon replaced by humility and self-deprecation during the week of her penitence. Her utter rejection of all that has been a part of her life to that point and her only desire being the hope of reconciliation with the true God paint a picture of the totality of her conversion experience. The passion that is evoked within Aseneth, by both Joseph *and* her desire to be reconciled to God, conveys a message that both love and allegiance to God are from heaven. Indeed, heaven smiles on love. (I'd really be worried if Aseneth were only converted to Joseph's famous good looks. I really want to see this guy. Does he have something over Donny Osmond?) The fact that Aseneth transfers this passion to God is a good sign. She needs to make a drastic change in her lifestyle and psyche. We expect something pretty dramatic in order for her to do this, and we definitely are *not* disappointed.

Aseneth's new name, "City of Refuge," is symbolic of the idea that all repentant souls will be protected and cherished by God. The promises made to her remain available to *all* of the penitent. Burchard points out that this portrayal of a woman in a role often occupied by men may also reflect the fact that more women than men became full proselytes and that a relatively liberal status was bestowed upon women in some sectors of Jewish Hellenism.[10]

Aseneth's actions of entering into a period of fasting, confession, prayer, meditation, washing, a symbolic changing of clothes, the receipt of a new name, and the eating of a special meal all suggest some type of ritual involved in her conversion. We hear echoes of covenantal language here. However, as the text stands, Aseneth's conversion is purely a personal affair.

As Aseneth's is "no ordinary conversion," she does not marry an ordinary man. "Joseph is the prototype of the persecuted and exalted righteous man."[11] He is portrayed as being sensitive to the point of prescience, as a result of being endowed with the Spirit of God (4:8, 6:1–7, 19:4). His glorious appearance is reminiscent of the stirring good looks of Adonis in Greek mythology. For such a "Powerful One of God" (18:1), a special bride is required. Aseneth becomes such a bride through the commission of the commander of the hosts of heaven. Aseneth's virginity, although she is an idol worshipper, is strongly emphasized, refuting the tradition that idolatry and sexual immorality go hand in hand.[12] The author must show that Aseneth the idolatress remains the virgin that will be worthy of marriage to the righteous patriarch Joseph.

As with other biblical epiphanies, the change of Aseneth's name to "City of Refuge" shows a change from individual to matriarchal status.[13] The character of Aseneth is elevated to archetypal standing, and this woman, who has sought refuge, becomes a city of refuge to others (13:12, 15:7). She becomes "the prototype of proselytes," and her immortality is promised to all who follow her example.[14] She attains the status of Abraham as one who has left an idolatrous nation to come to know the one true God. In this sense, she becomes an *ezer* to all who seek to come to know the true God. She provides strength and inspiration to all seekers of truth and to all who attempt to change the directions of their lives.

Notes

1. In Genesis 41:45, the name of Joseph's wife is "Asenath." Throughout this chapter, I will use the spelling in the LXX and in the Greek text, "Aseneth."

All quotations from "Joseph and Aseneth" will be from C. Burchard's translation in *The Old Testament Pseudepigrapha,* Volume 2. Edited by James H. Charlesworth (Garden City: Doubleday, 1985).

2. The Targum of Genesis states, "And [Pharaoh] gave [Joseph] Asenath, who Dinah had borne to Shekem, and the wife of Potiphera prince (Rabba) of Tanis had brought up, to be his wife." J. W. Etheridge, *The Targums of Onkelos and Jonathan ben Uzziel on the Pentateuch* (London: Longman, Green, Longman, Roberts, and Green, 1865), 304.

3. Edith Hamilton, *Mythology* (New York: Little, Brown and Company, 1969), 121.

4. George W. E. Nickelsburg, "Stories of Biblical and Early Post-Biblical Times," in

Jewish Writings of the Second Temple Period. Edited by Michael E. Stone. (Philadelphia: Fortress Press, 1984), 67.

5. See Book of Jasher ch. XLIV in which Potiphar's wife, Zelicah, desires Joseph, and her friends cut their hands with knives as they are peeling citrons and gazing at Joseph's beauty. Book of Jasher (Salt Lake City: J. H. Parry & Company, 1887), 130.

6. Although Joseph's action could be construed as having sexual connotations, the integrity of his character makes such an interpretation improbable.

7. Adam instructs Eve to let no speech come out of her mouth as she does her penance in the Tigris River because her lips are unclean from partaking of the forbidden fruit. See *Vita Adae et Evae* 6:2 in M. D. Johnson's, "Life of Adam and Eve" in *The Old Testament Pseudepigrapha,* vol. 2. Edited by James H. Charlesworth (Garden City: Doubleday, 1985).

8. Nickelsburg notes that although Aseneth does not receive either bread or drink, perhaps one should think of heavenly manna as the bread and honey from the honeycomb as the drink. The imagery of food and drink has probably been developed as a parallel to the food and drink of an idolatrous cult. See "Stories of Biblical and Early Post-Biblical Times," 187.

9. C. Burchard, "Introduction to Joseph and Aseneth," in *The Old Testament Pseudepigrapha*, vol. 2. Edited by James H. Charlesworth (Garden City: Doubleday, 1985), 190.

10. Ibid.

11. Nickelsburg, "Stories of Biblical and Early Post-Biblical Times," 68.

12. See Numbers 25 and Hosea 1–3.

13. See Genesis 17:5,15; 32:28.

14. Nickelsburg, "Stories of Biblical and Early Post-Biblical Times," 69.

Chapter 5

New Girls on the Block

THE PSEUDEPIGRAPHA ARE REPLETE WITH golden nuggets of information about the women of the scriptures who were formerly nameless or relative unknowns. Because of these writings, we are now able to know them by name and perhaps understand the motivations for their actions.

Sitis, the Wife of Job

In the Book of Job in the Bible, we don't get much information about Job's wife. All we see is her bitter response to Job's suffering. She doesn't sound much like a woman of inspiration.

The account of Job's life begins with a conversation between Satan and God, which is an interesting scenario in and of itself. The sons of God come to present themselves before the Lord, and Satan also comes with them. Unlike the later Jewish and Christian portrayal of the devil, the Satan in Job is a member of God's heavenly council "whose functions are rather like those of a prosecuting attorney."[1] God points out to Satan that Job is righteous. "There is none like him in the earth, a perfect and an upright man, one that feareth God, and escheweth evil" (Job 1:8). Satan answers: "Doth Job fear God for nought? Hast not thou made an hedge about him, and about his house, and about all that he hath on every side? . . . But put forth thine hand now, and touch all that he hath, and he will curse thee to thy face" (Job 1:9–11). He is saying, "Of course Job is righteous and obedient. You are blessing him immeasurably in every arena. He knows where his bread is buttered. He only obeys because he has it so good. If things get tough, he won't be so quick to bless your name." God has great faith in Job's righteousness and allows Satan to afflict Job in all realms, with the exception of his physical body. He experiences the loss of all that he possesses. He loses his vast wealth and all of his children die. Either trial would have been devastating, but Job still praises the Lord: "The Lord gave, and the Lord hath taken away; blessed be the name of the Lord" (Job 1:21).

Satan again has a conversation with the Lord in which the Lord once more points out that Job is still faithful, even though he has lost everything. Satan answers by saying, in effect, "Maybe so, but you have not touched him personally. If you make him suffer, he will turn on you." God responds, "Have at it, but don't kill him." So Satan afflicts Job with boils, oozing sores from the crown of his head to the soles of his feet. He scrapes off the pus with a piece of a broken pot.

Job's wife watches him with amazement. She says to him, "Dost thou still retain thine integrity? curse God, and die" (Job 2:9). She cannot believe that her husband would stand by a God who has seemingly abandoned him. Surely God could heal him of the wretched boils! She tells him to quit being a foolish believer. Job's suffering seems to have broken her spirit.

In *The Testament of Job* in the pseudepigrapha, we get a totally different picture of Job's wife. First of all, she is given a name—Sitis. According to Job's account, he sits on a dung heap outside the city for forty-eight years with worms crawling on the boils of his body. Discharge from his sores wets the ground under him. If a worm falls off his body, he picks it up again and returns it to its place saying, "Stay in the same place where you were put until you are directed otherwise by your commander" (20:9). Sitis is driven by poverty to work as a slave in order to support her husband. Job is forced to watch as Sitis carries water into the house of a certain nobleman (no doubt one of his former counterparts) as a maidservant so that she might get bread and bring it to him. Job says, "The gall of these city fathers! How can they treat my wife like a female slave?" (21:3–4).

Before long, Job comes to his senses. When self-pity threatens to envelop him, and he approaches the point of despair, the compassionate actions of Sitis help him find hope. Realizing that he is loved by another makes all the difference to him, and he is able to endure. When he stops concentrating on himself and "begins to worry about his wife, his mind is restored." He takes charge of his emotions and gains the strength to fight his enemy.[2]

Job continues, "After eleven years they kept even bread itself from me, barely allowing her to have her own food. And as she did get it, she would divide it between herself and me, saying with pain, 'Woe is me! Soon he will not even get enough bread!' " (22:1–2).

Job relates that Sitis would not hesitate to go out into the market to beg bread from the bread sellers so she could bring it to him to eat. When Satan learns of this, he disguises himself as a bread seller. Sitis approaches him, thinking he is a man, and he says to her, "Pay the price and take what you like. She answers, 'Where would I get money? Are you unaware of the evils that have befallen us? If you have any pity on me, show mercy.' " Satan replies glibly, "Unless you deserved the evils, you would not have received them in return. Now then if you have no money at hand, offer me the hair of your head and take three loaves of bread. Perhaps you will be able to live for three more days" (23:1–7).

The shaving of one's head in the *Testament of Job* is not a sign of grief but of disgrace. First Corinthians 11:6 reads, "For if the woman be not covered [veiled], let her also be shorn: but if it be a shame for a woman to be shorn or shaven, let her be covered."[3] Sitis has apparently reached a point where she no longer cares what people think. She answers the bread seller, "What good is the hair of my head compared to my hungry husband?" (23:8). And so, showing disparagement for her hair, she tells the man to go ahead and take it. He takes out scissors and cuts off her hair while all in the market are looking on, marveling, and he gives her three loaves of bread. After she receives the loaves, she sets out at once to bring them to Job. The text reads, "Satan followed her along the road, walking stealthily, and leading her heart astray" (23:11).

When she approaches Job, she cries out with tears saying,

> Job, Job, How long will you sit on the dung heap outside the city thinking, "Only a little longer!" and awaiting the hope of your salvation? As for me, I am a vagabond and a maidservant going round from place to place. Your memorial has been wiped away from the earth—my sons and the daughters of my womb for whom I toiled with hardships in vain. And here you sit in worm-infested rottenness, passing the night in the open air. And I for my part am a wretch immersed in labor by day and in pain by night, just so I might provide a loaf of bread and bring it to you. Any more I barely receive my own food, and I divide that between you and me—wondering in my heart that it is not bad enough for you to be ill, but neither do you get you fill of bread. (24:1–6)

She then tells Job of her painful experience in the marketplace and of her trading her hair for bread.

Following this recital of events, the author of the *Testament of Job* breaks into a lament for Sitis. This poetic dirge contrasts her former wealth and acts of charity to her present pitiful state:

> Who is not amazed that this is Sitis, the wife of Job?
> Who used to have fourteen draperies sheltering her chamber and a door within doors, so that one was considered quite worthy merely to gain admission to her presence:
> Now she exchanges her hair for loaves!
> Whose camels, loaded with good things, used to go off into the region of the poor:
> Now she gives her hair in return for loaves!
> Look at her who used to keep seven tables reserved at her house, at which the poor and the alien used to eat:
> Now she sells outright her hair for loaves!
> See one who used to have a foot basin of gold and silver, and now she goes along by foot:
> Even her hair she gives in exchange for loaves!
> Observe, this is she who used to have clothing woven from linen with gold:
> But now she bears rags and gives her hair in exchange for loaves!
> See her who used to own couches of gold and silver:
> But now she sells her hair for loaves! (25:1–8)

After reading this tragic lament, the reader cannot help but be filled with compassion for this wonderful woman who has now been reduced to such a sorry state. Sitis next utters a statement parallel to the one she makes in Job 2:9 when she says, "Job, Job! . . . In the weakness of my heart, my bones are crushed. Rise, take the loaves, be satisfied. And then speak some word against the Lord and die" (25:9–10). Carol Newsom observes, "Job's wife is the one who recognizes, long before Job himself does, what is at stake theologically in innocent suffering: the conflict between innocence and integrity, on the one hand, and an affirmation of the goodness of God, on the other."[4]

Job answers her, "Why have you not remembered those many good things we used to have? If we have received good things from the hand of the Lord, should we not in turn endure evil things? Rather let us be patient till the Lord, in pity, shows us mercy" (26:4–5). This reply is similar to the one in the Bible. However, in this pseudepigraphical book, Job adds an insight that explains why such a formerly strong and faithful woman would momentarily falter. He says, "Do you not see the devil standing behind you and unsettling your reasoning so that he might deceive me too?" (26:6). Job challenges Satan to come out of hiding and fight him directly.

Satan then comes out from behind Sitis, and Job confronts him head-on. They struggle with each other, like two athletes wrestling. Satan pins Job, and Satan fills Job's mouth with sand to silence him. But Job refuses to give in to defeat, enduring all the punishments inflicted upon him. In the end, Job conquers Satan through his patient endurance (27:1–6). Although Satan has been successful in torturing Job with excruciating pain, Job maintains his integrity throughout his silent suffering. And what of Sitis? How much of Job's endurance did she enable or even facilitate?

In the Bible account, Job's reproof of his wife is the last thing he says for quite a while. Newsom points out that "when he finally speaks in [Chapter] 3, his words sound distinctly like those of his wife. Though he does not exactly curse God, he curses the day of his birth. Though he does not die, he speaks longingly of death. . . . His wife's troubling questions have become his own."[5] Sitis has moved Job to be honest.

The next chapters in the *Testament of Job* deal with the lament of Job's friend Eliphas for Job, followed by the words of Baldad and Sophar. While they are speaking, Sitis arrives "in tattered garments, fleeing from the servitude of the official she served, since he had forbidden her to leave" (39:1–2). She throws herself at their feet and says while weeping, "Do you remember me . . . what sort of person I used to be among you?" She pleads with Job's friends to order their soldiers to dig through the ruins of the house that fell on her children so that at least their bones can be preserved as a memorial. Job tells them not to bother with this task since it will be in vain. "For you will not find my children, since they were taken up into heaven by the Creator their King" (39:12). Job's friends accuse him of being truly demented, but he asks them to help him stand up. He then sings praises to the Father and asked them to look up to the east and see "[his] children crowned with the splendor of the heavenly one" (40:3).

When Sitis sees this, she falls to the ground worshiping and says, "Now I know that I have a memorial with the Lord." She says she will arise and return to the city and nap for a while before returning to her duties of servitude. She goes to the cowshed of her oxen, which have been confiscated by the rulers whom she serves. She lies down near a certain manger and dies "in good spirits" (40:4–6).

Is Sitis an *ezer* according to the *Testament of Job*? Although her strength temporarily wavers because of Satan's powerful influence upon her, the portrait depicting a once-proud woman who sells her hair to rescue her suffering husband is powerful indeed. What would have happened to Job if she had not worked as a servant in order to feed him? It is certain that he would not have lived to have his blessings restored.[6]

Naamah—The Wife of Noah

In the text of Genesis, Noah's wife does not have a name. We can guess that, as the second "Eve," or mother of the human race, she must have been a special woman indeed. She had the faith to believe her husband had a call from God, although everyone around him must have thought he was crazy to build a boat in the middle of the desert!

Noah's wife is known as Naamah according to Jewish tradition. "Naamah was Noah's wife, and why was she called Naamah? Because her deeds were *neimim* (pleasing)."[7] This description of Naamah inspired one contemporary author, Sandy Eisenberg Sasso, to create a tale about just why Naamah must have been so pleasing. While Noah is given the task of gathering two of every type of animals to take aboard the ark, Naamah is called upon by God to gather the seeds of every type of plant upon the earth and bring them aboard the ark so that they might be saved from the flood. She is helped in her mission by a great wind that gathers the seeds of the giant redwoods and cedar trees. As she walks across the fields in her many-pocketed apron, she gathers the seeds of all the flowers, but she walks right past the dandelions, pretending not to notice them. God reminds her that she must gather the seeds of *every* living plant, and she reluctantly gathers them.

After the floods have receded and the land is dry and firm again, Naamah carefully takes out all the seeds and seedlings from the deep pockets of her apron and begins to plant them in the moist earth. Because she tried to ignore the dandelion, God makes sure they are everywhere.[8]

Louis Ginzberg collected many legends of the Jews and published them in a seven-volume set of books. He says this about Noah's wife:

It was by the grace of God, not on account of his merits, that Noah found shelter in the ark before the overwhelming force of the waters. Although he was better than his contemporaries, he was yet not worthy of having wonders done for his sake. He had so little faith that he did not enter the ark until the waters had risen to his knees. With him his pious wife Naamah, the daughter of Enosh, escaped the peril, and his three sons, and the wives of his three sons.

Noah had not married until he was four hundred and ninety-eight years old. Then the Lord had bidden him to take a wife unto himself. He had not desired to bring children into the world, seeing that they would all have to perish in the flood, and he had only three sons, born unto him shortly before the deluge came. God had given him so small a number of offspring that he might be spared the necessity of building the ark on an overlarge scale in case they turned out to be pious. And if not, if they, too, were depraved like the rest of their generation, sorrow over their destruction would but be increased in proportion to their number.[9]

Is Noah's wife an *ezer*? How can we learn from her example? Even if the Jewish legends about Naamah are fanciful, we can use our reason to conclude that Noah's wife was a very strong woman. Although she has been satirized by modern drama to be a gossip and a shallow individual, she must have endured a lot to be counted "righteous" enough by the Lord to warrant being one of only eight people to survive the flood. Although being married to a righteous man must have given her strength, it was no guarantee of salvation, as Lot's wife can confirm. She saved her family through her faith and belief in her ark-building husband, and she enabled the future of the rest of mankind after them.

Sambethe—Noah's Daughter-in-law

The *Old Testament Pseudepigrapha* contain several books of Sibylline Oracles. Sibylline Oracles were widely accepted as prophetic in the ancient world. The first attested "Sibyl," arising from the fifth to the fourth centuries B.C., was a single prophetic individual. Sibyl might have originally been the proper name of a prophetess. J. J. Collins states, "The Sibyl is always depicted as an aged woman uttering ecstatic prophecies."[10] Many cultures throughout the ancient world had Sibyls, and there have been various attempts throughout history to make lists of the various Sibyls. The number of women on these lists ranges from four to twelve. The Hebrew Sibyl is purported to be the daughter-in-law of Noah and is known as Sambethe or Sabbe.[11] There is no conclusive evidence to associate the name to any one origin. Michelangelo includes a Sibyl in his paintings on the ceiling of the Sistine Chapel.

The most prominent characteristic of a Sibylline oracle was a prediction of the distress and misery to come upon the world. Like the Old Testament prophets, they prophesied of war, famine, and pestilence that would come upon various groups of people, usually due to violations of the laws of the gods, or in the case of the Hebrew people, the commandments and statutes of Jehovah. Occasionally a glimmer of hope permeates the prophecies of doom, heralding a restoration of favor after the desolation has passed.

The idea that the Hebrew Sibyl was associated with Noah comes from the Third Sibylline Oracle: "God put all of the future in my mind so that I prophesy both future and former things and tell them to mortals. For when the world was deluged with waters, and a certain single approved man was left floating on the waters in a house of hewn wood with beasts, and birds, so that the world might be filled again, I was his daughter-in-law and I was of his blood."[12] What follows is the ultimate in journal keeping.

The Hebrew Sibyl praises God and denounces idolatry, chronicles the events of the tower of Babel, and predicts the downfall of Rome. She then lists the kingdoms of the earth in their turns—Egypt, Persia, Media, Assyrian Babylonia, Macedonia, and Rome. She speaks of a city in the land of Ur of the Chaldeans, where men are righteous and are concerned about "good and noble works" and a "prosperous man . . . gives a share of the harvest to those who have nothing" (lines 244–45). She tells of the exodus of the twelve tribes from Egypt and their restoration to their own land and the building of a temple. She tells of another exile to Assyria and the destruction of the beautiful temple. She speaks of a king[13] who will reign and a new temple that will be built. She recounts the woes that are to befall various nations—Macedonia, Rome, Troy, Greece, and many others. Then the creator of the earth "will set down much lamented fire on the earth. One third of all mankind will survive" (543–44).

She berates the people of Greece for thinking their mortal leaders can save them from death and their dumb idols can save them from destruction. She tells them they should "revere the name of the one who has begotten all, and do not forget it" (550). She tells of a "sacred race of pious men" that honors the Most High in his temple, and does not give honor to gold or silver idols of "dead gods" (587–88). These men "are also mindful of holy wedlock, and do not engage in impious intercourse with male children" (595–96). All those who "were not willing to piously honor the immortal begetter of all men, but honored idols" would suffer "war and pestilence and lamentable ills" (604–05). She speaks of the cosmic judgment of the whole earth, when the whole of creation will "shudder before the face of the Immortal" (679). "Rocks will flow with blood" (683–84), and there will be brimstone from heaven (691).

Then the Sibyl prophesies of the salvation of the elect who will "all live peacefully around the Temple" being shielded by the Creator "as if he had a blazing wall of fire round about" (702, 703, 706). The Sibyl exhorts the Greeks to live morally and reject abortion and homosexuality. "Shun unlawful worship . . . Avoid adultery and indiscriminate intercourse with males. Rear your offspring and do not kill it, for the Immortal is angry at whoever commits these sins" (763–66).

The Sibyl concludes by describing a millennial panorama: "All the paths of the plain rugged cliffs, lofty mountains, and the wild waves of the sea will be easy to climb or sail in those days, for all peace will come upon the land of the good. Prophets of the great God will take away the sword for they themselves are judges of men and righteous kings . . . Wolves and lambs will eat grass together in the mountains" (777–82, 788). Her last pronouncement is, "let all these things from my mouth be accounted true" (829).

If Sambethe is indeed a real person, she certainly shows strength in speaking out against the immorality she sees in the nations of the earth. She is called "a crazy liar" (816) for prophesying the things she foretells. It is never a pleasant task to point out the corruption in a society. People *hate* to be called to repentance. She asserts her legitimacy forcefully and leaves us with this message: "But when everything comes to pass, then you will remember me and no longer will anyone say that I am crazy, I who am a prophetess of the great God" (816–18).

Eluma—Mother of Samson

The rousing account of Samson relates an instance of a child being dedicated to the service of God by his mother. The narrative in Judges contrasts the righteousness of his Israelite mother with the unrighteousness of the three other women in his life, none of whom were of Israelite birth. The dramatic events associated with his birth foreshadow a remarkable destiny.

The Bible reports that an angel appeared to the wife of a man named Manoah, announcing that she would bear a child. Her name is Eluma, according to the pseudepigrapha. The angel directs her not to partake of the fruit of the vine, or of wine, and not to eat any unclean food and stipulates that her child shall observe the same regulations. In addition, he specifies that "no razor shall come on his head: for the child shall be a Nazarite unto God from the womb: and he shall begin to deliver Israel out of the hand of the Philistines" (Judges 13:5). This angel comes unbidden to Eluma, in contrast to other biblical women who plead with God for posterity.

Eluma runs to tell her husband about her encounter with the angel and says, "A man of God came unto me, and his countenance was like the countenance of an angel of God, very terrible: but I asked him not whence he was, neither told he me his name" (Judges 13:6). Manoah believes his wife's report but seeks further divine guidance about how to raise the child, who must be special indeed if his birth merits being announced by an angel from heaven. "Then Manoah intreated the Lord, and said, O my Lord, let the man of God which thou didst send come again unto us, and teach us what we shall do unto the child that shall be born" (Judges 13:8).

The Lord hearkens to Manoah's prayer and the angel reappears but comes only to Eluma as she sat in the field, not to Manoah. She rushes to find her husband and bring him to the man of God. Manoah asks, "How shall we order the child, and how shall we do unto him?" (Judges 13:12). The angel does not give any further guidelines about how the child should be raised, except to repeat the same dietary restrictions, adding only, "all that I commanded [the woman] let her observe" (Judges 13:14). Apparently, the angel felt that the primary responsibility for the righteous rearing of the child lay with his mother.

When the child is born, his mother gives him the name Samson. She, however, does not provide an explanation of *why* she chooses this particular name. Leila Leah Bronner writes the following about what Samson's name may mean: "It has been suggested that the Hebrew root *sh-m-sh*, can be understood as a diminutive form of the noun *shemesh*, or "sun," so that *Shimson* means "little sun."[14] One cannot help but wonder if his mother gives him that name because she anticipates his amazing strength and dauntless force.

Because mothers have always been particular about the women their sons find attractive, Eluma must have been sadly disappointed to see him overcome at the hands of the beautiful but calculating Delilah. In Hebrew, her name sounds like the word *lailah*, which means "night" or "darkness." In fact, when I was first learning Hebrew, I used Delilah's name as the pneumonic device to remember that new vocabulary word because she had a reputation of being a shady lady. The use of such symbolic names seems to foreshadow the conflict between light and darkness that will eventually cause the once-promising Samson to fall.

Undoubtedly, Samson's mother raises him according to the strict standards of Nazarite law and impresses upon him the grave responsibilities that come with being a Nazarite, or one whose life is dedicated to God. She must have taught him that the Lord's blessings are conditional upon obedience to God's law as well as obedience to the strict Nazarite law that he has adopted since his birth. She also certainly teaches him to live a holy life, so his desire to marry a Philistine woman must have seemed like an affront to his mother and the culture in which she had raised him. His parents, however they might object, cater to his selfish demands and obtain for him the wife he desires. Through the unhappy consequences of this inauspicious match, Samson engages in a reckless series of actions that result in hostility between the Israelites and the Philistines, who had been oppressing Israel for forty years at that time.

In his exploits against the Philistines, Samson becomes involved with three Philistine women—his wife from Timnah, a harlot from Gaza, and the crafty Delilah who eventually causes his demise. Conspiring to profit from his downfall, she ruthlessly tries three times to discover the secret of his amazing strength. She accuses him of not being sincere in his love for her and nags him so much that he finally succumbs to her and reveals that his strength comes from his stature as a Nazarite, one who has been dedicated to God's service "from [his] mother's womb" (Judges 16:17).

This mention of the womb brings to mind the unusual circumstances surrounding Samson's birth and his calling from a heavenly messenger. He has sadly disappointed God and his parents with his disregard for all that is holy. With his shorn hair, his great strength is gone from him, and the Philistines easily overcome him—making it the epitome of a "bad hair" day. They put out his eyes, and he is confined to the prison house while his hair slowly grows out again. In the final scene of the story, at a feast in the temple to the Philistine god Dagon, Samson makes one final plea to his God. "O Lord God, remember me, I pray thee, and strengthen me, I pray thee, only this once, O God, that I may be at once avenged of the Philistines for my two eyes" (Judges 16:28). He takes hold of two pillars that support the temple and brings them down with his newly restored strength. "And Samson said, Let me die with the Philistines. And he bowed himself with all his might; and the house fell upon the lords, and upon all the people that were therein. So the dead which he slew at his death were more than they which he slew in his life" (Judges 16:30). And so, Samson dies with the Philistines, which is sadly fitting since he had spent his life living *like* a Philistines.

The book of *Biblical Antiquities* in the *Old Testament Pseudepigrapha* adds many details to Eluma's story that are not present in the Judges narrative. First of all the author, Pseudo-Philo, tells us her name and tells us she is the daughter of Remac. He tells us that she is sterile and has not born any children to her husband Manoah before Samson.[15] But then the narrative takes a fascinating twist and gives us information about this couple's relationship that could have come straight from the twenty-first century. Apparently, Eluma does not appreciate her husband telling her every day, "Behold the Lord has shut up your womb so that you may not bear children, and now let me go that I may take another wife lest I die without fruit" (42:1).

Just as a modern woman might do today, Eluma stands up to her husband and challenges him, saying, "Not me has the Lord shut up that I may not bear children, but you that I may not bear fruit" (42:1). It is incredible that she, a woman in the patriarchal society of the ancient world, would accuse her husband of being the sterile one! Manoah expresses his frustration at this seemingly pointless argument: "Would that this could be tested and proved!" He would have been amazed that in our day such tests are routine and quite conclusive. The text continues, "And they were quarreling daily and both were very sad, because they were without fruit" (42:1).

Eluma decides that she needs to find out whether her husband's accusation is true or not, so she decides to ask God. "One night the wife went up to the upper chamber and prayed, saying, 'Behold you, Lord God of all flesh, reveal to me whether it has not been granted to my husband or to me to produce children, or to whom it may be forbidden or to whom it may be allowed to bear fruit in order that whoever is forbidden may weep over his sins because he remains without fruit. Or if both of us have been deprived, then reveal this to us also so that we might bear our sins and be silent before you" (42:2).

Eluma's words reveal that she is operating under several assumptions—one, that being unable to conceive a child has got to be the fault of either the husband or the wife, or perhaps both; and two, that being unable to bear children is the result of a judgment from God because of one's sins. Clearly, this woman is tired of arguing and wants an answer. She gets one delivered by the mouth of an angel: "The Lord heard her voice and sent his angel to her in the morning, and he said to her, 'You are the sterile one who does not bring forth, and you are the womb that is forbidden so as not to bear fruit. But now the Lord has heard your voice and paid attention to your tears and opened your womb.' " (42:3).

We are not told in the Bible that Eluma has shed tears because she has no children, but in *Biblical Antiquities*, the angel makes reference to them. The angel continues, "And behold you will conceive and bear a son, and you will call his name Samson. For this one will be dedicated to your Lord" (42:3).[16]

What we have here is an annunciation scene, much like the scene in which the angel Gabriel appears to Mary and informs her of the child she will bear and what his destiny will be. There are also many similarities to the annunciation of the birth of John the Baptist to Zacharias in the gospel of Luke. Both Christ's and John the Baptist's annunciations include a familiar pattern: sterility, prayer in seclusion, the appearance of the angel, and the announcement of what the name of the child is to be.[17] There are only a few annunciation scenes in the Bible, so it is probably safe to assume that the mother of Samson is indeed a righteous, specially chosen woman.

The angel tells Eluma that her child will be dedicated to the Lord as a Nazarite (from the word *nazar* meaning "separate")—a group that did not partake of the fruit of the vine, touch anything that was dead, or allow a razor to cut their hair (see Numbers 6:2–6). "But see that he does not taste from any fruit of the vine and eat any unclean thing, because (as he [presumably God] himself has said) he will free Israel from the hand of the Philistines" (42:3). After the angel leaves, Eluma goes into the house and tells her husband, "I am placing my hand upon my mouth, and I will be silent before you all the days because I have boasted in vain and have not believed your words. For the angel of the Lord came to me today and revealed to me, saying, 'Eluma, you are sterile, but you will conceive and bear a son' " (42:3).

Manoah's reaction is different here than it is in Judges, where he believes her words. In *Biblical Antiquities*, Manoah does not believe his wife. "Being perplexed and sad," he goes into the upper chamber of the house and prays, saying, "Behold I am not worthy to hear the signs and wonders that God has done among us or to see the face of his messenger" (42:5). While he is speaking, the angel appears again to Eluma who is in the field and says to her, "Run and announce to your husband that God has accounted him worthy to hear my voice." So Eluma runs to the house to get her husband, and he hurries to the angel in the field. The angel says to him, "Go into your wife and do all these things." Manoah replies, "I am going, but see to it, sir, that your word be accomplished regarding your servant." Clearly, he does not want a disappointed wife. The angel assures him, "It will be accomplished" (42:6–7).

Manoah next tries to persuade the angel to come home with him and have a meal, which he declines. Then Manoah builds an altar on a rock and cuts up meats and places them upon it to offer as a sacrifice. The angel then touches the sacrifice with the tip of his staff, causing fire to come forth from the rock and devour the sacrifice. The angel of the Lord "went up from thence with the flame of fire." When Manoah and his wife see these events, they fall on their faces and say, "Surely we will die because we have seen the Lord face to face" (42:8–10). (A widespread belief existed among the ancient Israelites that if a person saw God, or apparently even his messenger, he would die.)

We are told next that "Eluma conceived and bore a son and called his name Samson, and the Lord was with him" (43:1). The rest of the narrative about Samson and his exploits and unwise choices is parallel to the Judges account for the most part. In the concluding episode of Samson's life, the number of casualties from the collapse of the Philistine temple is increased to forty thousand. Apparently, Eluma and Manoah have other sons because the text concludes with the line, "And Samson's brothers and all the house of his father went down and took him and buried him in the tomb of his father" (43:8).

Looking back at the life of Samson, we see parallels between his life and the life of Christ. At first, this might appear ironic, even blasphemous, because of the stark differences in their characters. Jesus is sinless—Samson is anything but. In spite of their differences, like Jesus, an angel announces Samson's birth. The angel tells his parents that Samson will "*begin* to deliver Israel out of the hand of the Philistines" (Judges 13:5). Jesus's mission was to *finish* the job by delivering all of humankind out of the hands of sin and death.

Furthermore, Samson's wedding riddle alludes to the life of the Savior. It reads, "Out of the eater came forth meat, and out of the strong came forth sweetness" (Judges 14:14) and refers to the honey he finds in the carcass of a lion that he has killed with his bare hands. Maybe eating the honey lets Samson know that something good and sweet will come from the death and havoc he will inflict on the Philistines. The riddle itself alludes to the Savior in an Isaiah-like multifaceted way. The most powerful link is to the Savior's triumph over Satan and death. Out of Satan came forth death, but out of death comes something sweet. Nothing is sweeter than what is possible because of the Savior, and the Savior is stronger than Satan.

Next, both the Savior and Samson are betrayed. Delilah nags Samson to tell her the source of his strength until "his soul was vexed unto death" (Judges 16:16). Delilah wants the silver the Philistines have promised to her if she delivers a weakened Samson to them. His confiding in her could cause his death, but Samson does not seem to care. He tells her all his heart, his hair gets cut, he is surprised that the Lord is not with him, and he is taken by the Philistines who put out his eyes. The Savior is also betrayed for silver by someone close to him, and he is also surprised that God is not with him in the Garden of Gethsemane—perhaps with better reason, since the Savior has not betrayed a commandment as Samson has.

When Samson goes to Gaza to see a harlot, the Philistines are out to get him. They sleep by the city gate so they can capture him in the morning. At midnight, Samson pulls out the city gates, bar included, and carries them to Hebron, thirty-seven miles away. Hebron was the religious center for Israel at that time because Abraham had buried Sarah there. We can liken the gate to the cross the Savior bore to a hill near Jerusalem. The Savior destroys the gates of hell and opens the gates of heaven with his death on that hill. The Savior prays on the cross, and Samson prays in the temple of Dagon. They both pray for strength to finish the work they are sent to do. Like Christ, Samson saves his people through his death.

Both the Bible and *Biblical Antiquities* describe Samson's mother, Eluma, as a woman who is highly regarded by God. Like Aseneth and Mary, she is visited by a heavenly being. She is accounted worthy to receive *two* visits from the angel before her husband is judged worthy to receive *one*. In a society where patriarchal power is prevalent, she is deemed suitable to receive her own private revelation of divine will. In fact, it is Eluma who is told to fetch her husband to come and see the angel, not the other way around.

Does the mother of Samson meet the criteria to be regarded as an *ezer*? If one of the definitions of an *ezer* is to be strong, then Eluma certainly fits it well. She boldly stands up to her husband in refusing to be blamed for their lack of children. And yet when she learns that the failure to conceive is indeed her fault, she is quick to apologize to her husband for her "boasting" and her failure to heed his words. As all spouses know, it takes great personal strength to be able to do that. Also, even though Samson does not live up to the standards he was taught "from the womb," he *knows* from where his strength comes because he has been taught by a righteous mother. He confesses to Delilah, "I have been a Nazarite unto God from my mother's womb: if I be shaven, then my strength will go from me, and I shall become weak, and be like any other man" (Judges 16:17). Eluma can always be comforted with the knowledge that she was counted worthy by God to be given the calling to raise a potential judge in Israel *no matter what choices Samson made.* I think other righteous mothers who have taught their children well, only to have them stray from the desired path, should remember the example of Eluma. She performs her duty; Samson does not. His downfall comes because he does not live up to his privileges, not because of anything his mother does or does not do. I'm sure his actions brought her great sorrow, but she can stand strong, knowing that she taught him well.

The Mother of Seven Sons in 4th Maccabees

Another exemplary woman is the mother of seven sons in *4th Maccabees* in the *Old Testament Pseudepigrapha*. She doesn't have a name in this book, but is known in Jewish tradition as Hannah or Miriam bat Tanhum.[18] She is an inspiring example to any mother who strives to encourage her children to be faithful to their beliefs, no matter what oppression may come because of it.

The story begins with the author telling his audience why he is writing his story. He poses a philosophical question: "Is reason the master of passion?" He defines reason as "the mind making a deliberate choice of the life of wisdom," wisdom being "knowledge of things divine and human." He asserts that the two major kinds of passion are pleasure and pain. He submits that reason is indeed the master of passion and supports his view by recounting the story of a woman who has seven sons.

I need to explain the political background of the story before its nuances will be clear. After the death of Alexander the Great, his empire is divided between his four generals. General Seleucus is assigned to rule the area of Syria, which includes Jerusalem. The Jews in Jerusalem resist his rule and refuse to worship Greek gods. After Seleucus dies, his son Antiochus Epiphanes becomes the political ruler. Epiphanes means "manifest" [as a god] and he rules from 175–164 B.C. He has an unpredictable character—sometimes being generous to a fault, and at other times brutally tyrannical. Polybius, a Greek historian, gives him the nickname Epimanes ("utterly mad") because of his "instability verging on insanity."[19] His treatment of the Jews is excessively harsh. He hopes to use the common culture of Hellenism to unite the various cultures in the Seleucid empire. After a humiliating defeat in Egypt,

Antiochus returns to Jerusalem determined to enforce his policy of Hellenization upon the Jews, "even to the extent of completely exterminating them and their religion."[20]

Antiochus dispatches his tax collector with twenty-two thousand men to attack Jerusalem on the Sabbath. Most of the men of the city are killed, and the women and children are enslaved. Afterward, all Jewish practices are forbidden, and a monthly inspection is made. Any Jew possessing a copy of the Book of the Law or any child that has been circumcised is put to death. Women are hurled from walls along with their circumcised infants.[21] The sacred temple is rededicated to the god Zeus, and pagan sacrifices are offered on the altar to Zeus, which had been built over the altar of the temple.[22]

The tyrant Antiochus Epiphanes surrounds himself with fully armed troops and tries to force every Hebrew to eat swine's flesh and food sacrificed to idols. Whoever does not eat this "defiled food" is tortured and put to death. The first man brought forth is an old man of priestly lineage named Eleazar. Antiochus says to him, "Before I have the tortures begin on you, old man, I would advise you to eat of swine's flesh and save yourself . . . Consider this also, that even if there is some power that watches over this religion of yours, it would pardon you for any transgression committed under compulsion" (5:6,13). Eleazar replies, "We, Antiochus, who firmly believe that we must lead our lives in accordance with the divine Law, consider that no compulsion laid on us is mighty enough to overcome our own willing obedience to the Law" (5:16). Then Antiochus's guards strip the old man of his clothes and scourge him with whips.

When Eleazar can endure the pain no longer, he falls to the ground. Then, partly out of pity and partly out of admiration for his courage, some of the king's courtiers approach him and say, "Why, Eleazar, are you so unreasonably destroying yourself in this foul way? Let us bring you some of the cooked food, and you pretend to taste of the swine's flesh and save yourself" (6:14–15). Eleazar cries aloud, "It would most surely be contrary to reason if, having lived our lives in accordance with the truth right up to our old age and having preserved our fair reputation for so living in conformity with the Law, we should now change and ourselves become a model of impiety to the young by setting them an example of eating unclean food" (6:18–20). Because of his bold rejection of their offer of mercy, they bring him to the fire, throw him in, and pour a foul-smelling concoction into his nostrils. There he perishes, but, to the end, he affirms his dedication to the Law.

As the mother and her seven sons watch Eleazar's torture, she speaks to them in the Hebrew tongue: "My children, noble is the struggle, and since you have been summoned to it to bear witness for our nation, fight zealously for our ancestral Law. Shameful were it indeed that this old man should endure agonies for piety's sake, while you young men were terrified of torments. Remember it is for God's sake you were given a share in the world and the benefit of life, and accordingly you owe it to God to endure all hardship for his sake" (16:16–19). She then cites the faith of the prophet Abraham who was willing to sacrifice his son Isaac, who in turn "did not flinch" when his father's hand, with knife in it, fell down against him. She also speaks of Daniel, who was thrown in a pit with lions, and of Hananiah, Azariah, and Mishael who were cast into the fiery furnace, and "all endured for the sake of God." She continues, "Therefore, you who have the same faith in God must not be dismayed. For it would be unreasonable for you who know true religion not to withstand hardships" (16:20–23).

Having been thwarted in his first attempt to force the old man to eat unclean food, Antiochus, "in a violent rage," orders other Hebrew captives to be brought forth. He says that if they eat of the food, they will be released, but if they refuse, they will be even more savagely tortured. Seven brothers, along with their aged mother, are brought forth, "handsome and modest and well-born and altogether charming" (8:3). Antiochus is struck by them and "astounded by their comeliness and nobility." He smiles at them and tells them that he wants to show them favor and, not only promises them freedom if they partake, but tells them they will "receive leading positions of authority over [his] domain" (8:4–7). He continues, "Share in the Greek style, change your mode of living, and enjoy your youth. If you provoke me to anger by your disobedience, you will compel me to the use of dreadful punishments to destroy each and every one of you by torture" (8:8–9).

Then Antiochus brings forth his instruments of torture in order to terrorize the young men into eating of the unclean food. "The guards then brought forward the wheels and joint dislocators, racks and wooden horses [probably a bone crushing device of some sort], catapults

69

and cauldrons, braziers and thumbscrews, iron claws and wedges and bellows" (8:12–13). But, rather than pragmatically rationalizing their behavior and acting to save their lives, they cry with one voice and say, "Why do you delay, tyrant? We are prepared to die rather than transgress the commandments of our forefathers. . . . Do not think that you can harm us with your torments. By our suffering and endurance we shall obtain the prize of virtue and shall be with God, on whose account we suffer" (9:1–9).

Furious at hearing these words, Antiochus brings forth the oldest son, rips off his tunic, and begins flogging him. When the young man acts as if the flogging made no impression on him, they put him on the wheel and begin to put his limbs out of joint. As limb after limb is broken, he cries, "Sever my limbs, burn my flesh, twist my joints, and through all these torments I will prove to you that the children of the Hebrews alone are invincible in the defense of virtue" (9:17–18). When they hear this, they draw the wheel tighter and put the fire under him. The wheel is smeared with his blood, the fire steams with the discharged fluid dropping down upon it, and bits of flesh spin around on the axles of the machines, and still the youth does not let out so much as a groan. Throughout all this torture, the mother urges him on to death for piety's sake. Just before his death he cries out, "Imitate me, my brothers. . . . Fight the sacred and noble fight for true religion" (9:23–24).

The plight of the second son is much the same, except he is fastened to the torture machine with iron hands that rip off all the skin from his cheeks and from his head. He courageously endures this agony and says, "How sweet is every kind of death for the sake of our ancestral religion" (9:29). Once again, his mother urges him on in the Hebrew tongue to remain true to his faith.

When the third son is brought forth, the people fervently admonish him to partake of the food and save himself. He cries aloud and says, "Do you not know that the very same father begot both me and my dead brothers, and the same mother bore us all, and I was brought up on the same doctrines? . . . Therefore, if you have any means of torture, apply it to my body, for my soul you cannot touch even if you would" (10:2–4).

The author of *4 Maccabees* praises the mother by saying, "O piety that was dearer to the mother than her sons! When two options lay before her, namely piety or the instant deliverance of her seven sons according to the tyrant's promise, she loved piety better" (15:2–3). The author continues with his adulation: "Indeed, because of her sons' moral heroism and their willing obedience to the Law, she cherished an even greater love for them . . . Nevertheless, although all the many promptings of maternal love pulled the mother toward the bond of affection for them, in not a single case did their varied tortures avail to sway her reason, but each and every child and all of them together did the mother urge on to death for piety's sake" (15:9, 11).

When the fourth son is brought forward, the guards say to him, "Do not you, too, show the same madness as your brothers, but obey the king and save yourself." But he replies, "For me you cannot heat the fire so hot as to make a coward of me" (10:13–14). On hearing this, Antiochus orders that the boy's tongue be cut out. The boy taunts him with the cry that God will speedily overtake him because he was "cutting out the tongue that sang songs of praise to him" (10:21). Still, the mother continues to strengthen her sons. When he, too, dies, the fifth son springs forward and says, "I waste no time in demanding the torture for virtue's sake, but of my own accord come forward that you might kill me" (11:2–3). They bind his knees to the catapult with iron cramps, after which "they twisted his loins back over the circular wedge until he was curled back on the wheel like a scorpion and his limbs were all disjointed. And thus, struggling for breath and racked in body," he says, "A glorious favor you bestow on us, tyrant . . . enabling us as you are to manifest our constancy toward the Law" (11:10–12). Still the mother remains valiant. The author states: "With what a manifold host of torments then was the mother tortured while her sons were racked by the wheel and fire. But in the midst of her passionate feelings pious reason nerved her whole being with a manly courage and enabled her to transcend the immediate affections of a mother's love" (11:22–23).

When the fifth son dies, the guards bring forward the sixth son who is "a mere lad." The tyrant asks if he is willing to "eat and be released." But he replies, "I am younger in age than my brothers, but just as old in reason. We were born and reared for the same purpose, and we are likewise obliged to die in the same cause. Accordingly, if you want to torture me for not eating unclean food, do your torturing now" (11:13–17). They stretch him out on the wheel until his backbone is disjointed and then set a fire under him. Heating up sharp skewers, they run them into his back and burn out his entrails. But under all this torture he declares, "Six of us, lads though we are, have destroyed your tyranny . . . Your fire is cool for us and your catapults painless and your violence powerless" (11:24–26).

When he dies, the seventh and youngest son comes forward. Antiochus is "moved with pity" when he sees this young boy, and tries to persuade him to save himself by saying, "You see the outcome of your brothers' folly . . . And you, too, if you refuse to obey, will be miserably tortured and will yourself meet a premature death. But if you do obey you will be my friend and will be given charge over my affairs of state" (12:3–5). Hoping to appeal to him by speaking such words, he sends for the boy's mother "so that he might show pity to her over the loss of so many sons and further urge" her remaining son to obey and save himself. After all, he is the sole surviving son and has the responsibility of caring for his mother in her old age. But, when the mother arrives, "she [gives] her son encouragement in the Hebrew tongue" to stand by his ideals and maintain his integrity just as his brothers have (12:6–7).

After hearing his mother's words, the son asks to be loosed that he might speak to the king. The guards gladly do so, hoping that he might obey and escape torture. However, he runs to the nearest brazier and addresses Antiochus, saying, "Impious man, of all the wicked ones you most ungodly tyrant, are you not ashamed to receive your kingdom with all its blessings from the hand of God and then to kill those who serve him and torture those who practice piety? . . . Are not you, who are but a man, ashamed, you savage beast, to cut out the tongues of men who share the same feelings as you and are made of the same elements and to torture them in this brutal fashion? . . . You will groan dreadfully for having slain the champions of virtue without cause" (12:11–14). When he is on the "point of death," he declares, "I shall not prove deserter to my brothers' valor" (12:15–16). He then throws himself into the braziers and ends his life.

After thus chronicling the account of the death of the seven sons, the author of *4 Maccabees* launches into a panegyric of their mother.

He says, "For the mother of the seven youths endured the agonies inflicted on every one of her children. Consider how tangled is the web of a mother's love for her children so that her whole feeling is the profoundest inward affection for them" (14:12–13). The recitation of her praise continues:

> She saw the flesh of her children melt away in the fire and their toes and fingers scattered on the ground, and the flesh of their heads right down to the cheeks laid out before her like masks. O mother, sorely tried now by pains sharper than the pains of birth! O woman who alone among women brought perfect piety to birth! . . . When you saw your children's flesh burned on children's flesh, and severed hand upon hand, and flayed head upon head, and corpse fallen upon corpse, and when you saw the place crowded with spectators of your children's torments, you did not weep. Not the sirens' melodies nor the sweet sound of the swan's song so charm the hearers' ears as do the children's voices charm their mother when they speak to her from amid the tortures. (15:15–17, 20–21)

He describes her piety as stronger than the song of the sirens, whose song no human can resist. The Greek word used to describe this inner strength is *andreiosas* or "manliness." She hears the tortured cries of her sons, and—despite feeling their agony in every recess of her soul—she remains strong and does not succumb to her motherly feelings.

The author goes on to compare her to Abraham, who was willing to sacrifice his only son. Seldom does a woman gain the comparative status of a patriarch in ancient literature. "In the council chamber of her own heart, so to speak, she saw clever advocates, nature and parenthood and maternal love and the torment of her children—a mother holding two votes in regard to her children, one to consign them to death and the other to preserve them alive; but she did not decide on the safe course that would preserve her sons for a little while, but like a true daughter of God-fearing Abraham called to mind Abraham's unflinching bravery" (15:25–29).

The author of *4 Maccabees* goes on to elevate her to a privileged status by comparing her to other heroes of Judaism. Robert Darling Young points out that since she acts like Abraham, she is relegated to a similar place in the spiritual history of Israel, as reflected in the names the author uses to describe her in his eulogy. She is addressed as "mother of the nation," "champion of the Law," "defender of piety," and "prize-winner in the inward contest of the heart." She is described as "more noble than men in fortitude and stronger than heroes in endurance" (15:29–30). She is compared to the ark of Noah because she is "buffeted on every side in the flood of passions," and yet is still able to weather the storms that beset her for the sake of her religion.[23]

The author next records a speech he feels that the mother *might* have spoken. In it, she bewails her fate. She laments that she is stripped of children and grandchildren and that she does not even have a descendant to bury her when she dies. Yet she does not give such a "dirge," nor urge any of her sons to avoid death, nor even grieve over them when they die. The author calls her a "holy and God-fearing mother" who with her "mind of adamant" brought her sons from "birth into immortal life." He describes her as a "soldier of God in piety's cause" and says that in deeds as well as words she is "stronger than a man" (16:5–15). With unwavering strength, the mother encourages each of her sons to die rather than transgress the commandments of God. Because of her inspiration, "they knew full well themselves that those who die for the sake of God live unto God" (16:25), apparently referring to their "speedy journey to heaven after their martyrdoms."[24]

When the mother is about to be seized and put to death, she throws herself into the fire so that no one will touch her body. The author concludes with a line of praise: "Be of good cheer, therefore, mother of holy soul, whose hope of endurance is secure with God. Not so majestic stands the moon in heaven as you stand, lighting the way to piety for your seven starlike sons, honored by God and firmly set with them in heaven. For your childbearing was from our father Abraham" (17:4–6).

Perhaps more distinctly than in any preceding passage, we can see here that the mother in *4 Maccabees* is squarely correlated to Abraham because she has borne her children in faith. Like Abraham's seed, who are as numerous as the stars in heaven, she and her sons are "firmly set with them in heaven." In addition, like Abraham, she was willing to obey a commandment from God that involved the sacrifice of her children. No wonder this author calls her a woman "whose soul was like Abraham's" (14:20). Certainly, she lives up to the highest purposes for which woman was created in the beginning. She is definitely an example of an *ezer*, whose great strength radiated into the hearts of her sons. She encourages them to plumb the depth of their own fortitude for the strength they need to endure anguish for the sake of holiness.

Notes

1. Carol Newsom, "Job" in *The Women's Bible Commentary*. Edited by Carol A. Newsom and Sharon H. Ringe. (Westminster: John Knox Press, 1992), 130–31.

2. Kenneth Hanson, *Secrets From the Lost Bible*, (San Francisco: Council Oak Books, 2004), 131–32.

3. "The disgrace might arise from cropped hair as (1) a mode of humiliating punishment (Aristophanes, *Thesmophoreazusae* 838: for rearing a cowardly son; or, Tacitus, Germania 19: for adultery) or (2) the practice of female homosexuals (Lucian, *Dialogi meretricli* 290 = 5.3)." See R. P. Spittler, "Testament of Job" in *The Old Testament Pseudepigrapha*, vol. 1. Edited by James H. Charlesworth (New York: Doubleday, 1983), 849.

4. Newsom, "Job," 132.

5. Ibid.

6. R. P. Spittler, "Testament of Job" in *The Old Testament Pseudepigrapha*, vol. 1. Edited by James H. Charlesworth (New York: Doubleday, 1983), 1:863 fn. 44e.

7. Bereshit Rabba 23:3 in Sandy Eisenberg Sasso, *A Prayer for the Earth: The Story of Naamah, Noah's Wife* (Woodstock: Jewish Lights Publishing, 1996), 3.

8. Sandy Eisenberg Sasso, *A Prayer for the Earth: The Story of Naamah, Noah's Wife* (Woodstock: Jewish Lights Publishing, 1996), 28.

9. Louis Ginzberg, *Legends of the Jews*, vol. 1 (Baltimore: The Johns Hopkins University Press, 1998), 159–60.

10. J. J. Collins, "Sibylline Oracles" in *The Old Testament Pseudepigrapha*, vol. 1. Edited by James H. Charlesworth (Garden City: Doubleday, 1985), 317.

11. Ibid., 317–18.

12. Ibid., 380, lines 821–27.

13. She is probably referring to Cyrus.

14. Leila Leah Bronner, *Stories of Biblical Mothers: Maternal Power in the Hebrew Bible* (Lanhan: University Press of America, 2004), 28.

15. Manoah's extensive genealogy is also given. "Now there was a man from the tribe of Dan whose name was Manoah, son of Edoc, son of Odon, son of Eriden, son of Fadesur, son of Dema, son of Susi, son of Dan." (Biblical Antiquities 42:1).

All quotations from Pseudo-Philo's Biblical Antiquities are from *The Old Testament Pseudepigrapha*, vol. 2. Edited by James H. Charlesworth. (Garden City: Doubleday, 1985).

16. Pseudo-Philo may have had in mind a derivation from the Hebrew *šmš* ("minister," or "serve") because of Samson's Nazarite status. Ibid. 356, n. 42f.

17. D. J. Harrington, "Pseudo-Philo's Biblical Antiquities" in *The Old Testament Pseudepigrapha*, vol. 2. Edited by James H. Charlesworth. (Garden City: Doubleday, 1985), 355, n. 42a.

18. Robin Darling Young, "The 'Woman with the Soul of Abraham': Traditions about the Mother of the Maccabean Martyrs," in *Women Like This: New Perspectives on Jewish Women in the Greco-Roman World*. Edited by Amy-Jill Levine. (ACLS Humanities E-Book, 1997), 67.

19. See "Antiochus" in *Anchor Bible Dictionary*, vol. 1. Edited by David Noel Freedman (New York: Doubleday, 1992), 270.

20. Ibid.

21. H. Anderson, 4 Maccabees in *The Old Testament Pseudepigrapha*, vol. 1. Edited by James H. Charlesworth (Garden City: Doubleday, 1985), 551 v. 4:25.

22. Ibid., 4:21.

23. Young, "The 'Woman with the Soul of Abraham': Traditions about the Mother of the Maccabean Martyrs," 77.

24. Ibid., 78.

CHAPTER 6

Seila: A Willing Sacrifice
Judges 11

THE STORY OF THE DAUGHTER of Jephthah in the book of Judges is one of the most tragic accounts in scripture. The biblical account is bewildering and raises many theological questions about the nature of God's love and his power over suffering. The extra-canonical versions of this tale offer new insights into how Jephthah and his daughter relate to other pivotal narratives in the Bible.

Jephthah is described as a "mighty man of valor" but one of disreputable heritage. His family tree reads like a modern-day soap opera. Judges 11 tells us that Jephthah is the son of a harlot. His father, Gilead, already has a wife and other sons, who in time cast Jephthah out. They say, "Thou shalt not inherit in our father's house; for thou art the son of a strange woman" (Judges 11:2). Jephthah grows up away from his people in the land of Tob and gains a reputation for being a bold warrior. He is powerful and ferocious enough that when the Gileadites need a brave fighter to lead them against the Ammonites in battle, they come to Jephthah, seeking his leadership. He reminds them of their past brutality to him, and he makes them promise that if he and the Lord prevail over the Ammonites, the Gileadites will make him their captain. Perhaps his great desire for the power that such a victory would bring motivates him to make the brash vow to the Lord that he next makes: "And Jephthah vowed a vow unto the Lord, and said, If thou shalt without fail deliver the children of Ammon into mine hands, then it shall be, that whatsoever cometh forth of the doors of my house to meet me, when I return in peace from the children of Ammon, shall surely be the Lord's, and I will offer it up for a burnt offering" (Judges 11:30–31). The record says that Jephthah slew the Ammonites in "twenty cities . . . with a very great slaughter. Thus the children of Ammon were subdued before the children of Israel" (Judges 11:33). Returning home with the flush of victory upon him, he no doubt seeks to share his joy with his family.

> And Jephthah came to Mizpeh unto his house, and, behold, his daughter came out to meet him with timbrels and with dances: and she was his only child; beside her he had neither son nor daughter. And it came to pass, when he saw her, that he rent his clothes, and said, Alas, my daughter! thou hast brought me very low, and thou art one of them that trouble me: for I have opened my mouth unto the Lord, and I cannot go back. And she said unto him, My father, if thou hast opened thy mouth unto the Lord, do to me according to that which hath proceeded out of thy mouth; forasmuch as the Lord hath taken vengeance for thee of thine enemies. (Judges 11:34–36)

In the portrait of Jephthah's daughter found in *Biblical Antiquities*, Pseudo-Philo expands the basic components of the biblical narrative and introduces other concepts. He focuses on her calamity and examines the various meanings it elicits. Through his interpretation of her tragedy, he confers upon her sacrifice an unparalleled significance and gives her life and death unique meaning.

Except for the basic points of the story, *Biblical Antiquities*[1] portrays Jephthah differently than the author of Judges does. Pseudo-Philo omits the reference to Jephthah's ignoble parentage but explains that his brothers banished him because they "envied him" (39:2). Evidently, he did not want to represent Jephthah as anything but a total Israelite. The book portrays him as a "mighty warrior" whom the Israelites seek out to lead them in battle (39:2–3ff).[2] They say to him, "Come rule over the people. For who knows if you have been kept safe to these days or freed from the hands of your brothers in order that you may rule your people in this time?" Such language is reminiscent of Mordecai's words to queen Esther when he says, "Who knoweth whether thou art come to the kingdom for such a time as this?" (Esther 4:14).

One of the major differences in the *Biblical Antiquities* version of this story is that Jephthah comes to the Israelite people as a prophet, admonishing them to repent and reminding them of God's mercy and willingness to forgive them and save them from their enemies. After gathering the people together, he says, "Now therefore set your hearts on the Law of the Lord your God, and let us beg him together, and so we will fight against our enemies, trusting and hoping in the Lord that he will not deliver us up forever. Even if our sins be overabundant, still his mercy will fill the earth" (39:6). The people repent and pray that God will deliver them. "Look, Lord, upon the people that you have chosen, and may you not destroy the vine that your right hand has planted" (39:7).

In the Pseudo-Philo account, Jephthah still makes a vow to God before going into battle, although in different words. "Jephthah rose up . . . to go out and fight in battle array, saying, 'When the sons of Ammon have been delivered into my hands and I have returned, whoever meets me first on the way will be a holocaust to the Lord' " (39:10). God responds to Jephthah's vow with anger: "Behold Jephthah has vowed that he will offer to me whatever meets him first on the way; and now if a dog should meet Jephthah first, will the dog be offered to me?" (39:11). God's wrath is kindled because Jephthah has been so vague in the wording of his vow. Jephthah's carelessness could result in the offering of something unclean according to the law of Moses.

God is justifiably infuriated with Jephthah. He has a good reason to be. However, God's next pronouncement catches us off guard. We might expect him to take his anger out on Jephthah, but God takes a different approach. He declares, "And now let the vow of Jephthah be accomplished against his own firstborn, that is, against the fruit of his own body, and his request against his only-begotten" (39:11). God is angry with Jephthah, but it is not Jephthah who will suffer. It is his *daughter* who will lose her life. We are left to wonder why Pseudo-Philo would choose to portray God in this seemingly inexplicable way. This shift points to a crucial component in the presentation of the story.[3]

God's mandate that Jephthah would sacrifice his own daughter relates back to the story of Abraham and Isaac in Genesis 22. "In both cases," Cheryl Ann Brown writes, "God is accountable for the sacrifice of the child." Each child is very dear to his or her father. Each is a willing sacrifice. In fact, Jephthah's daughter herself refers back to Isaac's example as an ideal of what her own response should be to the news of her destiny. She says to her father, "And who is there who would be sad in death, seeing the people are freed? Or do you not remember what happened in the days of our fathers when the father placed the son as a holocaust, and he did not refuse him but gladly gave consent to him, and the one being offered was ready and the one who was offering was rejoicing?" (40:2). In fact, there are parallels to Isaac's story in the wording of God's edict. Pseudo-Philo employs three expressions to portray Jephthah's daughter—"firstborn," "fruit of his own body," and "only-begotten." Only this last designation is used in the text of Genesis. The term "firstborn" connects Jephthah's daughter with Isaac, for he was Abraham's "firstborn" and heir, even though he was not the first son born to him. The second phrase, "fruit of his own body," is used by Pseudo-Philo elsewhere in *Biblical Antiquities* when he refers to Isaac (32:2, 4). The third phrase "only-begotten" is found in Hebrew in both Judges 11:34 and Genesis 22:2. Such a child is both unique and especially precious. One cannot help thinking of references to Christ in the New Testament, especially in the gospel of John, that refer to the Savior as God's Only Begotten.

Brown points out another interesting detail found in the Pseudo-Philo account:

> After declaring that Jephthah will sacrifice his daughter, God adds a pledge: "But I will surely free my people in this time, not because of him [Jephthah], but because of the prayer that Israel prayed" (39:11). This introduces an element not present in the Bible. Israel will be liberated not because of Jephthah, but because of Israel's prayer. This alone is what moves God to act on behalf of the people, not overzealous leaders who make rash vows and thus treat lightly God's holiness.[4]

The narrative of *Biblical Antiquities* briefly follows the battle with the Ammonites. Then it moves swiftly to the tense moment in which

Jephthah meets his cherished daughter. Because he does not realize that God has predetermined who will meet him, Jephthah becomes weak when he sees who has come. However, he quickly gathers his wits together to be able to tell his daughter what is to become of her.[5] "Rightly was your name called Seila, that you might be offered in sacrifice. And now who will put my heart in the balance and my soul on the scale? And I will stand by and see which will win out, whether it is the rejoicing that has occurred or the sadness that befalls me. And because I opened my mouth to the Lord in song with vows, I cannot call that back again" (40:1).

This pseudepigraphical account differs markedly from the biblical account, in which Jephthah initially reproves his daughter for being the one to meet him and then expresses his deep sorrow over his great dilemma. In the *Biblical Antiquities* account, Jephthah begins his speech by announcing his daughter's name for the first time—Seila. (Pseudo-Philo often names previously unnamed biblical figures in *Biblical Antiquities*.) The name Seila is derived from the Hebrew root *s'l* which means "ask." Seila is, therefore, the one "asked for" or "requested." It can also mean "to lend," or "to dedicate," as Hannah uses it in 1 Samuel 1:28: "I have lent him to the Lord; as long as he liveth he shall be lent to the Lord." If we see Seila's name as meaning she has been dedicated to the Lord, there is even greater evidence of her role as a female counterpart to Isaac, who was also dedicated to the Lord.[6] Pseudo-Philo asserts that Seila's offering was willingly given, as was Isaac's offering, and so was "acceptable." Later the Lord says "her death will be precious before me always" (40:3–4).

According to Pseudo-Philo, Jephthah's oath was unalterable because it was *God* who swore that Seila be sacrificed. The premise that God is the architect of Seila's destiny is the central focus of this text. When Seila learns of her father's vow, she needs to decide what her response will be. In Judges, she says, "My father, if thou hast opened thy mouth unto the Lord, do to me according to that which hath proceeded out of thy mouth; forasmuch as the Lord hath taken vengeance for thee of thine enemies" (Judges 11:36). Pseudo-Philo expands this brief statement in *Biblical Antiquities* to reveal the nature of Seila's character: "And who is there who would be sad in death seeing the people freed? Or do you not remember what happened in the days of our fathers when the father placed the son as a holocaust, and he did not refuse him but gladly gave consent to him, and the one being offered was ready and the one who was offering was rejoicing? And now do not annul everything you have vowed, but carry it out" (40:2).

Seila immediately accepts her fate, recognizing the parallel between her life and Isaac's. Just as Isaac's willingness to be sacrificed gave his offering significance and impact, so does Seila's free-will offering give worth to her own sacrifice.[7] She makes one request of her father—that she be allowed to go to the mountains with her friends to "bewail [her] virginity" for two months (Judges 11:37). Pseudo-Philo broadens this appeal to include the mourning of nature over the loss of her young life: "Yet one request I ask of you before I die, a small demand I seek before I give up my soul: that I may go into the mountains and stay in the hills and walk among the rocks, I and my virgin companions, and I will pour out my tears there and tell of the sadness of my youth. And the trees of the field will weep for me, and the beasts of the field will lament over me" (40:3).

The mention of her sadness might at first seem incongruous because she has just affirmed her willingness to be sacrificed, but upon further examination we see that grieving does not necessarily signal hesitancy. Clearly, her next words indicate that she does not lament the fact that she must die: "For I am not sad because I am to die nor does it pain me to give back my soul, but because my father was caught up in the snare of his vow" (40:3). Seila deplores the sin of her father and what must take place because of his foolish oath. In the next part of the narrative, God speaks on behalf of Seila, confirming that she definitely has to die, but applauds her for being "wise in contrast to her father and perceptive in contrast to all the wise men who are here" (40:4).[8]

Pseudo-Philo next presents the picture of Seila as a virgin weeping because she will never be a bride. This entire lament is not present in the biblical account, nor is it included in any other piece of extracanonical literature. She first implores all nature to listen to her lament and mourn with her. She explains her fate and her determination to sacrifice herself willingly so that "not in vain [would her] life be taken away":

Behold how I am put to the test!
But not in vain will my life be taken away,

May my words go forth in the heavens,
and my tears be written in the firmament!
That a father did not refuse a daughter whom he had sworn to sacrifice,
that a ruler granted that his only daughter be promised for sacrifice.
But I have not made good on my marriage chamber,
and I have not retrieved my wedding garlands.
For I have not been clothed in splendor . . . .
I have not used the sweet-smelling ointment,
And my soul has not rejoiced in the oil of anointing that has been prepared for me. (40:5–6)

Here Seila lists all the things she will never experience because of her offering. We see all of these things listed in detail, almost as if we are seeing her look through her hope chest and feeling the pain she must feel as she examines each item.

Seila next speaks to her mother:

O Mother, in vain have you borne your only-begotten daughter,
because Sheol[9] has become my bridal chamber,
though my people dwell on earth.[10]
And may all the blend of oil that you have prepared for me be poured out,
and the white robe that my mother has woven, the moth will eat it.
And the crown of flowers that my nurse plaited for me for the festival, may it wither up;
and the coverlet that she wove of hyacinth and purple in my woman's chamber, may the worm devour it.
And may my virgin companions tell of me in sorrow and weep for me through the days. (40:6)

Pseudo-Philo uses moving imagery here. Again, Seila is referred to as an "only-begotten" daughter. This reminds us of the magnitude of her parents' grief at having to let her go and also of her role as a female counterpart to Isaac.

The biblical account in Judges states that after Seila returned to her father, "he did with her according to his vow which he had vowed: and she knew no man" (Judges 11:39). Some have speculated that Seila did not die but was offered to the Lord and remained unmarried her whole life, because the text does not explicitly say that she was killed. According to *Biblical Antiquities*, the option for this interpretation no longer exists. Pseudo-Philo spells out in detail what Jephthah did: "and he did everything that he had vowed and offered the holocausts." He describes how "all the virgins of Israel gathered together and buried the daughter of Jephthah and wept for her" (40:8). Both the Bible and Pseudo-Philo recount that these young women also established a practice of meeting every year on the anniversary of her death to mourn for her for four days (see Judges 11:39–40; *Bib. Ant.* 40:8). The pseudepigraphical account also adds that Seila's tomb carries her name. Instead of remaining the nameless biblical figure in Judges, she is kept alive through a yearly festival, and she is honored at a tomb that bears her name. She becomes, in *Biblical Antiquities*, a significant figure in her own right, not just the daughter of one of the minor judges of Israel.

Seila is the preeminent figure in the story. The story of Jephthah diminishes into the background as Pseudo-Philo explores the meaning of her willing sacrifice. He interprets Seila's sacrifice as a counterpart to Isaac's willing sacrifice. He emphatically declares that it is *God* who demands the sacrifice, that Seila's death is for the benefit of the people, and that her death is precious before God always.[11] Her offering has value because, by it, the people are freed.

Is Seila an *ezer* as she is portrayed by Pseudo-Philo? In the account of Abraham in Genesis 22, we see a parallel between Abraham and the Father of us all. We see the pain that Abraham goes through as he attempts to obey God's mandate to sacrifice his "only-begotten." So too the Father of the Only-Begotten must have agonized over the necessity of his own son being offered. With Abraham being so advanced in years, he would not have been able to bind young Isaac had Isaac not been *willing* to be bound. Seila was also willing to give herself to the Lord. Therefore, is Seila not also a type of the Only Begotten who was sacrificed that his people might be freed from sin and death? Is this not the epitome of what being an *ezer*—a savior and a deliverer—is all about? I feel excitement and validation that God would see fit to provide a female type for the sacrifice of his Son included in scripture. It is there in the book of Judges, but we have to ponder and meditate on the meaning of the story to see the correlation. Pseudo-Philo thought that such an insight was too important to miss and has spelled it out for us clearly in *Biblical Antiquities*. This is just one more reason why I love these pseudepigraphical texts.

Notes

1. Biblical Antiquities in *The Old Testament Pseudepigrapha*, vol. 2. Edited by James H. Charlesworth (Garden City: Doubleday, 1985).

All quotations from Biblical Antiquities used in this chapter are from this translation.

2. Cheryl Ann Brown, *No Longer Be Silent: First Century Jewish Portraits of Biblical Women* (Louisville: Westminster/John Knox Press, 1992), 95–96.

3. Brown, *No Longer Be Silent: First Century Jewish Portraits of Biblical Women*, 97.

4. Ibid., 98–99.

5. Ibid., 100.

6. Ibid., 101–102.

7. Ibid., 103.

8. Ibid., 104, 108.

9. *Sheol* is Hebrew for "the world of spirits."

10. Translation from the Latin text by Brown in Brown, *No Longer Be Silent: First Century Jewish Portraits of Biblical Women*, 110.

11. See Brown, 125.

Chapter 7

The Women Who Rescued Moses
Exodus 1–24

THE STORY OF MOSES, ISRAEL'S paramount prophet, cannot be told without including the crucial women in his life. Moses' life is literally saved many times by these strong women—first by the midwives at his birth, then by his mother and sister, and then by the daughter of Pharaoh. Later, as a grown man, his wife, Zipporah, saves his life by performing a religious ritual. All these women bless the life of Moses and enable him to fulfill his divine destiny.

Shiphrah and Puah—the Hebrew Midwives

Many centuries after the prophet Joseph wielded his influence in Egypt, the children of Israel grew into a formidable force in the land. The king of Egypt became fearful of their numbers and devised a wicked scheme to limit their population growth. The story is found in Exodus 1:15. It begins when the king calls in the two Hebrew midwives and commands them to kill all of the male babies that they deliver. The girls will be allowed to live.

The verse begins, "And the king of Egypt spake to the Hebrew midwives." The language of this verse is ambiguous: "Hebrew midwives" could mean "midwives who are Hebrew" or "midwives to the Hebrews." The ambiguity leaves open the possibility that these women are Egyptian. Verse seventeen offers further reason to question. It says, "the midwives feared God." If the midwives are Hebrew, this detail might seem unnecessary. But since there is some doubt about their heritage, it is possible that they are Egyptian women who are ordinarily not "God-fearing" but are stirred by the spirit against this evil plot. Regardless of their heritage, these women feel that murdering the very newborns they labor to bring into the world would be morally wrong. Such actions run contrary to their maternal natures. They are heedless of the fact that a person in power is speaking to them as subordinates. If they refuse to obey, they may be imprisoned, punished, or killed, yet these midwives show courageous defiance.

The names of these two fearless midwives, Shiphrah and Puah, have been preserved in the Bible for all generations to revere. These names are associated with valor, courage, and moral integrity. The preservation of their names in scripture is a way to pay tribute to their memory and honor them as valiant women who put their lives on the line to do the right thing.

In Exodus 1:16, the king says, "When ye do the office of a midwife to the Hebrew women, and see them upon the [birthing] stools; if it be a son, then ye shall kill him: but if it be a daughter, then she shall live." It is a mystery how the king thinks his heinous scheme will remain undiscovered. Won't the Hebrew mothers soon figure out that their male babies are being born dead when the midwives assist them? Won't they quit calling on these midwives if their presence is associated with stillbirths? We can't be sure, but it is possible that if half the Hebrew babies are born alive (the girls), the mothers will not be as apt to detect that anything is wrong. Because the Hebrews live in slavery and under oppression, the infant mortality rate may already be high—perhaps already near fifty percent. In such circumstances, the Hebrew mothers will not readily make the connection that the stillbirths are all boys and the live births girls. In the meantime, the king will have partially succeeded in his plan for exterminating the Hebrews.[1]

One rabbinic commentator explains that the Pharaoh's desire to destroy all male Hebrew babies probably originated when his astrologers foretold that a male who had not yet been born was destined to be the future deliverer of the Hebrew people.[2] The king would certainly feel compelled to prevent the Hebrew people's liberation. Considering the king's clear motivation, these women who refuse to obey his specific order are indeed heroic. They take great risks to ensure that *all* Hebrew babies are born alive. They must be brave women of strong moral fiber to act in a manner exactly opposite to their orders.

The rabbinic commentaries add more details about the actions of these brave women. Not only do they *not* kill the male infants, they go above and beyond their responsibilities as midwives. They knock on the doors in Hebrew neighborhoods to gather the food needed by new mothers.[3] When they are confronted with a difficult birthing situation, they petition God to help them. When they have a baby that is in danger of being strangled by the umbilical cord or in a dangerous position or in some other life-threatening situation, they turn to God in mighty prayer: "Master of the Universe, You know that we have transgressed the edict of the Pharaoh. It is *Your* will that we seek to uphold. Oh, Creator of the Universe, please allow this newborn to emerge whole and perfect."[4]

On the day that Moses is born, the astrologers declare, "Today was born the deliverer of the Hebrews! But we do not know whether the deliverer is Egyptian or Hebrew. However, we can foresee that this redeemer's end will be caused by water."[5] Consequently, the king commands that everyone, even the Egyptians, must drown their newborn sons. It is interesting to note that the astrologers can not perceive clearly whether the redeemer is an Egyptian or a Hebrew. Looking back historically, the reason they could not discern the nationality of the redeemer seems obvious. Moses is both Hebrew *and* Egyptian. He is born of Hebrew slaves but is rescued and raised as an Egyptian by the Pharaoh's daughter.

A rabbinic commentator notes that the Egyptian people balk at the command to kill their own children. They cannot believe that the redeemer of the Hebrews will be an *Egyptian*. Surely he will be a Hebrew![6]

At some point before the drowning, Pharaoh comes to suspect that the midwives have not been following his orders. In Exodus 1:18–19 he calls them before him and asks: "Why have ye done this thing, and have saved the men children alive?" The midwives certainly must be afraid for their safety at receiving such a summons. They could be chastened, imprisoned, or even executed for their insubordination. They have come prepared with an explanation. They answer, "Because the Hebrew women are not as the Egyptian women; for they are lively, and are delivered ere the midwives come in unto them." The word translated as *lively* comes from the Hebrew word *chayot* which contains the familiar Hebrew word *chai* or "life." The word *chayot* is often translated as "wild creature." They told the Pharaoh that while the Egyptian women require the assistance of a midwife, the Hebrew women give birth before the midwives arrive to help them. Thus, they are able only to help with the delivery of the afterbirth and to assist the new mothers with their own needs.

Jochebed

In the book of Pseudo-Philo in the *Old Testament Pseudepigrapha*, the text states that "Amram of the tribe of Levi went out and took a wife from his own tribe." Amram and his wife had one son and one daughter and "their names were Aaron and Miriam. And the spirit of God came upon Miriam one night, and she saw a dream" (9:9–10). Miriam recounts the dream to her parents the next morning. She says that she saw a man in a "linen garment" who stood and spoke to her. He told her to give her parents the following message: "Behold he who will be born from you will be cast forth into the water; likewise through him the water will be dried up. And I will work signs through him and save my people, and he will exercise leadership always" (9:10). Her parents do not believe her.

Traditionally, Miriam has been associated with the title "the prophetess." Although we do not have this dream recorded in the Bible, Jewish tradition reflects the belief that Miriam has special gifts.

After Jochebed gives birth to her healthy son, she undoubtedly fears for his life. The scriptures tell us that she is able to hide him for three months. Commentary by a Jewish rabbi provides more detail about Jochebed's efforts to hide her baby. She makes a secret dugout under the floor of her house and lines it with blankets.[7] By placing her baby in this hiding place, she is able to delude the Egyptian police when they come to search for Hebrew newborns.

Another commentator relates the methods of these Egyptian patrolmen. They would surround the home of every Hebrew woman of childbearing age, and, blocking the exits, force their way inside. The soldiers would bring an Egyptian baby with them on these operations, and they would then force the infant to cry, hoping to discover a secreted Hebrew child who would instinctively wail in response and betray his hiding place.[8]

After three months Jochebed realizes she needs to take further action to protect her child. She cannot hide her infant from the Egyptian militia any longer. She weaves a basket of reeds in order to float the baby to safety. In *The Complete Works of Josephus*, Josephus states that Amram, the baby's father, has a dream in which he learns that his son is the promised deliverer of his people. Amram shares the dream with Jochebed, saying, "This child of thine . . . shall be concealed from those who watch to destroy him: and when he is brought up in a surprising way, he shall deliver the Hebrew nation from the distress they are under from the Egyptians." Jochebed and Amram determine "to intrust the safety and care of the child to God, [rather] than to depend on [their] own concealment of him, which [they look] upon as a thing uncertain, but [they believe] that God [will] some way for certain procure the safety of the child, in order to secure the truth of his own predictions."[9]

Jochebed knows that even if Moses's basket manages to float, there is a great chance of his being noticed and killed. She takes every precaution to ensure his survival. The Bible text of Exodus 2:3 tells us that she daubs the basket with hardened mud and pitch to prevent water from entering and causing it to become submerged. She herself does the building, the weaving, and the sealing. She places the basket in the river. A rabbinic commentator says that this was normally a man's work but that Jochebed does it even more skillfully than a man can. She weaves the ark from the tall reeds that grow along the riverbank, so that it will be camouflaged once she launches it among them. Jochebed's actions, according to Rabbeinu Bachya, are devised to satisfy the astrologers' predictions that the prophesied redeemer will die by water. She will leave him in the water just long enough that, if her son *is* the predicted deliverer, the soothsayers will perceive that their projections have come to pass, and the Pharaoh will retract his decree. Because the astrologers' wizardry is not completely definitive, Jochebed is hoping that they will only recognize that the baby is in the Nile and not that the boy is still living. Then she can go back to the river and rescue her baby in secret.[10] Her strategizing indicates that she has all the makings of a great lawyer.

After she places Moses in the river, Jochebed commissions Miriam to watch over her brother, standing "afar off" (Exodus 3:3). If she herself is unable to rescue her baby, Jochebed hopes that a compassionate Egyptian woman will take pity on the Hebrew boy and raise him as her own. It is likely that she has Miriam watch over Moses so that she can observe and describe the method of his deliverance. Jochebed has faith that her son has been foreordained for a higher mission and that the Lord himself will provide a way to save the child.[11] And provide a way he does—through the compassion of the Pharaoh's own daughter.

The Daughter of Pharaoh

Just as Amram and Miriam have prophetic dreams, so also—it seems—does the daughter of Pharaoh. "Now Pharaoh's daughter came down to bathe in the river, as she had seen in dreams" (Pseudo-Philo

9:15). It seems that, according to Jewish tradition, her finding the boy baby is far from a random coincidence. The Bible continues, "And the daughter of Pharaoh came down to wash herself at the river; and her maidens walked along by the river's side; and when she saw the ark among the flags, she sent her maid to fetch it. And when she had opened it, she saw the child: and, behold, the babe wept. And she had compassion on him, and said, This is one of the Hebrews' children" (Exodus 2:5–6).

In their book *Moses' Women*, Shera Aranoff Tuchman and Sandra E. Rapoport include several additional details from various rabbinic commentators. Through these commentaries we learn that the day is scorching hot, and the princess has come down to the river to gain a respite from the heat by bathing in the cool water. We also learn that the Pharaoh's daughter may have a chronic skin rash that is irritated by the hot-water baths in the palace. Consequently, the princess routinely visits the cooling waters of the river every morning to get relief from her ailment. Tuchman and Rapoport further note that it is indeed miraculous that the princess comes down to the river in a semi-public place to bathe, as decorum would dictate that she bathe in private. It is also miraculous that the lady-in-waiting that accompanies the princess to the water is her lifelong servant, whose humble standing and loyalty to her mistress would guarantee that she would not question the princess's actions. It could have been perilous for the princess and for the baby had *any* other person witnessed the princess's discovery.[12]

The commentaries further point out that the princess must feel a great deal of inner turmoil upon finding the basket. As a daughter of the king, she has grown up with unquestioning loyalty to her father's decrees. Now, all of a sudden, she is faced with the "up close and personal" effects of one of those edicts—a reed basket which contains one of the doomed Hebrew babies. She has to make a decision in that moment that will change her life forever. Should she rescue the poor soul from certain death and defy her father's explicit orders? The Bible describes her reaching toward the basket as she hears the baby's cries. One rabbinic commentator relates that as she reaches out her hand to grab the side of the floating basket, the sores on the princess's skin are healed. This miracle astounds her, and she immediately resolves to save the life of the baby boy in the ark. At this point, the commentators call the princess by a new name: "Batya." Translated from the Hebrew, this name means "daughter of Jehovah." Batya has chosen to let the compassion aroused in her by a helpless baby boy govern her actions instead of the fear of her father's reprisals against her.[13]

One commentary compares Pharaoh's daughter's lifting the baby out of the waters of the Nile to the act of giving birth. She delivers him from the waters that could have caused him to lose his life at any moment. Without her intervention, the fate of the Hebrew baby boy would have been, in all probability, tragic. Batya's act of recovering Jochebed's basket "is as vital . . . as [his mother's] act of giving the baby life. Both acts gave life to Moses."[14]

As the princess looks inside the ark, she sees that it contains a baby *boy*. The baby is circumcised, leading the princess to conclude that he is a sequestered Hebrew baby who has been launched onto the water. The Bible first uses the word *yeled*, derived from the verb meaning "to give birth," to refer to the baby. The second Hebrew word, translated as "babe," is *na'ar*, which is usually translated as "lad," but can refer to any male from infancy to adolescence. Rabbinic commentary explains that when the Pharaoh's daughter opens the basket, she assumes it will contain a two-day-old baby and is surprised to see a three-month-old infant! She is amazed that this boy's mother has been so successful in hiding him from the king's troops for so long. She concludes that the Hebrew mother must have been clever indeed.[15]

The princess is facing a pivotal crisis—how can she act in a charitable manner towards this helpless infant and simultaneously *not* disobey her father's mandate? If she rescues the boy, her father will hear of it and may have her killed. Even if she is able to conceal the baby at first, raising him in the palace in secret will be near impossible.[16] One commentary solves this problem by speculating that the princess feels she is not actually breaking the letter of her father's command. His decree is to throw the Hebrew male babies *into* the river. The baby's mother had technically conformed to this directive when she placed her son in the water in his floating ark.[17]

There are amazing parallels between the birth of Moses—as told in the Bible and other writings—and the birth of Jesus in Matthew 1, including communication by dreams, prophecy about a future mission, the need for concealing the infant, and the killing of male babies. Jesus is strikingly cast a man "like unto" Moses.[18]

Miriam

Miriam is the next female in Moses's life that saves him through courageous acts: "Then said [Miriam] to Pharaoh's daughter, Shall I go and call to thee a nurse of the Hebrew women, that she may nurse the child for thee? And Pharaoh's daughter said to her, Go. And the maid went and called the child's mother" (Exodus 2:7–8).

Miriam must have great courage in order to be able to approach the daughter of the Pharaoh. They are clearly *not* on the same social plane, and her approaching the princess during her personal reverie is presumptuous to say the least. According to rabbinic commentators, Miriam's inborn courage is amplified by God, who supplies the boldness necessary for Miriam to approach the princess. Her courage is also bolstered by having closely followed what is happening on the riverbank from her hiding place in the bulrushes. When Miriam sees the daughter of Pharaoh's tenderhearted reaction to the baby, she is "emboldened to reveal herself."[19]

After Miriam offers to find a Hebrew woman to nurse the child, the princess readily answers in the affirmative. We might wonder why the princess is so eager to have a *Hebrew* wet nurse instead of an Egyptian one. An Egyptian authority has explained that Miriam's question causes the Pharaoh's daughter to appraise, in a moment, who would be the best nurse for the child. Even if she would have been more comfortable with an Egyptian wet nurse, Miriam's idea of a *Hebrew* woman is more logical because an Egyptian servant will probably feel duty-bound to obey the king's overriding order to kill the child. The princess does not want to risk the chance and so agrees to the Hebrew nurse.

The Bible tells us that Miriam's intent all along is to go and bring the her mother, who has been absent from him for only a few hours.

One commentator, the Netziv, offers evidence of Miriam's wisdom by pointing out the repetition of the Hebrew word *lach* meaning "for you" in verse 7: "Shall I go and call a nurse of the Hebrew women *for you*, that she may nurse the child *for you*?" The commentator concludes that Miriam understands that if a Hebrew girl and a Hebrew woman are accessories in saving a young Hebrew male, they will be on very dangerous ground. However, if the girl obtains a Hebrew nurse *in the name of the princess* ("for you") and if that Hebrew woman is to nurse the child at the request of the princess ("for you"), both the girl and the woman will be safeguarded. The resolution that the baby Moses will be nursed by his own birth mother is clearly astounding and miraculous. Although he will grow up in the courts of Pharaoh, he will also have an awareness of his Hebrew roots.[20]

Exodus 2:9–10 reads, "And Pharaoh's daughter said unto her, Take this child away, and nurse it for me, and I will give thee thy wages. And the woman took the child, and nursed it. And the child grew, and she brought him unto Pharaoh's daughter, and he became her son."

We can only imagine the joy that Jochebed feels when Miriam returns home with the news of Moses's rescue and the request to come immediately to the banks of the Nile, where she is to meet the daughter of Pharaoh. Jochebed must know immediately that this tenderhearted princess is indispensable to her son's survival. When the princess says, "Take this boy and nurse him *for me*," it is clear that the king's daughter already has maternal feelings for this Hebrew baby. Moses is rescued, nursed by his own mother, adopted into royalty, and catapulted into greatness all because his sister, Miriam, handles a complicated situation with daring and shrewdness.[21]

When Jochebed returns two years later to give her son to the daughter of Pharaoh, her heart must harbor ambivalent feelings. She must be glad that he will not be raised as a slave but as an Egyptian prince. Although she will miss him, she must be grateful that he is alive. One Jewish commentator, the Malbim, notes that "it is part of divine providence" that Batya has not had second thoughts and is still eager to raise Moses as her son. Another points out that the princess has made two great sacrifices by her actions on the banks of the river. First, she has defied her father (the most powerful political leader in the world) by saving a Hebrew baby from death. Second, she must have realized that when she handed the child back to Jochebed, she would never *really* be the child's mother. He is hers only temporarily.[22]

The Bible recounts that after Jochebed brings her son to Pharaoh's daughter, *the princess* names him. "And she called his name Moses: and she said, Because I drew him out of the water" (Exodus 2:10). A Hebrew commentator says that "Moses" is a Hebrew translation—untranslated, his name is "Minius." Batya names him because it is she that has saved him from drowning in the river. The name that the princess gives Moses will stand as evidence that she is his second mother. Another commentator adds that Moses's name is humbling to him because it reminds him that he was taken from the waters by his adoptive mother. Moses is a unique combination of humility and dignity, as the son of a slave woman and the son of a princess.[23]

There is an oft-repeated midrashic story that tells just how assimilated Batya and her son are in Pharaoh's court. It is apparently a common practice for the princess to bring the child Moses to sit with her father while he is holding court in his throne room. The young boy is engaging and has, at a young age, charmed the entire court, including the Pharaoh. One day, in a capricious spirit, the toddler Moses grabs the crown from Pharaoh's head and puts it on his own head. The entire court looks on with consternation, and the Pharaoh's fortune-tellers take it as a sign that the adopted son of the princess is envious of the empire. They want the king to slay the boy to keep him from seizing the crown when he becomes a man. The Pharaoh is not inclined to accept their advice because, as the commentary says, he dotes on the boy like a grandfather. This midrash is based upon the assumption that Batya introduces Moses at court as her own son and that Pharaoh accepts him as such, treating him with special deference.[24]

The rabbinic commentator Sforno has stated that Moses's name is not meant to memorialize his origins but is meant to project his future role as a deliverer. Just as Moses is "pulled from the waters" and saved from inevitable death, so also is he decreed to "deliver other souls from suffering." Another expert explains that his growing up as a royal prince is part of divine design and is necessary to his development as a leader to myriads of people. As a result of his royal education, Moses acquires an aptitude and temperament far above that of the Hebrew slaves. The children of Israel require a leader who they can look up to with veneration and respect expressly because he has *not* been raised as a slave.[25] Miriam's role in helping the princess adopt Moses is vital to what he accomplishes later as an instrument in God's hands.

Zipporah

Exodus 2:11–15 recounts in a few abbreviated phrases that it is Moses's defense of a Hebrew slave and his subsequent slaying of that slave's taskmaster that prompt his flight from Egypt. He has committed treason against Pharaoh and will be killed on sight. It doesn't help his case that his actions have surely reminded Pharaoh of the predictions about the Hebrew deliverer. As both a Hebrew and an Egyptian who has just acted out in defiance, Moses fit the bill to be the fulfillment of this prediction more than ever, and he will have to be eliminated if he does not leave.

After fleeing Egypt, Moses reaches the land of Midian and sits down by the public watering hole. Here we again see a common biblical boy-meets-girl scene. Just as Abraham's servant finds Rebecca at a well and Jacob meets Rachel at a well, Zipporah and Moses also find this setting to be the ancient equivalent of "match.com." As he sits, Moses observes seven young women approaching the well. Exodus reads, "Now the priest of Midian had seven daughters: and they came and drew water, and filled the troughs to water their father's flock" (2:16). As Moses watches, other shepherds come and try to drive the young women away, but he—ever the defender of the weak—helps them water their flock. When Reuel, their father, asks them why they have returned so soon from watering the flock, they reply, "An Egyptian delivered us out of the hand of the shepherds, and also drew water enough for us, and watered the flock" (Exodus 2:19). Perhaps Moses's accent, manners, or dress reveal to them that he is an Egyptian. Reuel, or Jethro as he was also known, asks why they have left the stranger alone and tells them to invite the man back to their tent for dinner. "And he said unto his daughters, And where is he? why is it that ye have left the man? call him, that he may eat bread" (2:20). One rabbinic commentator says that when her father directs it, it is Zipporah who runs from the tent and dashes back to the well to invite Moses to her home.[26]

The next verse in the Bible tells us that "Moses was content to dwell with the man: and he gave Moses Zipporah his daughter" (2:21). Clearly, more has occurred during the visit than is recorded in Exodus. The first word in this verse in Hebrew is *vayoel*, which can be translated as "he consented" or "he swore." Rabbinic commentary is quick to fill us in on what Moses consented to and what his oath was. The commentary suggests that Reuel and Moses spent the night in a deep conversation. The conversation concludes with Reuel inviting Moses to stay with him for an extended visit and Moses offering to marry one of Reuel's daughters. Moses agrees to shepherd Reuel's many flocks. As a condition of Reuel's giving Zipporah to Moses as a bride, he requires Moses to swear that he will never leave to go to Egypt without first asking for his father-in-law's permission. Perhaps he wants to avert a repeat of the episode of Jacob leaving his father-in-law, Laban, without any notice. Moses takes the oath and is true to his word, asking and receiving Reuel's blessing before returning to Egypt years later.[27]

In her book, *Leave Her Alone*, Megan McKenna explores what happens next. Zipporah and Moses marry. She is a daughter of the priest of Midian. Moses, too, is from a priestly family of the tribe of Levi. Both Moses and Zipporah are priests according to the understanding of the ancients. Zipporah bears her husband a son. Moses names him Gershom, which means "sojourner." They live among the Midianites, who are also descendants of Abraham (see Genesis 25:2). Reuel teaches Moses about the traditions of Abraham and his faith in the one true God. Zipporah teaches Moses the art of shepherding, for this is a new vocation for him. After all, what is an ex-prince of Egypt qualified to do? It must require patience on his part to be taught by a woman when he has been a master of men. No wonder the Bible tells us that Moses is the meekest of men (Numbers 12:3). We can picture Zipporah teaching him her knowledge of the best grazing lands, the location of water sources, dangers from wild animals, as well as dangers from other nomadic tribes and bandits. She introduces him to the solitude of the desert, to the "isolation of tending sheep," and to the songs and prayers of the people of God. Moses learns to be a shepherd of the flocks of Reuel—one day he will shepherd the sheep that belong to Yahweh.[28]

The biblical text tells us that after Moses's experience at the burning bush, he returns to Midian with his flocks. Upon his return, he is met by Reuel; by his oldest son, Gershom; and by his wife, Zipporah, who is about to give birth to their second son. She was pregnant when Moses left months before to find rich pastureland for Reuel's flocks. Now, Moses has received a call from God to return to Egypt, and he is unsure whether he will ever return to Midian. He says to Reuel, "Let me go, I pray thee, and return unto my brethren which are in Egypt, and see whether they be yet alive. And [Reuel] said to Moses, Go in peace" (Exodus 4:18). Moses has just enough time to see his second son come into the world, obtain sanction from Reuel to leave Midian, and prepare his wife and sons to leave for Egypt. He has a mission and there is no time to waste.[29]

Before long, Moses, Zipporah, and their two sons set off for Egypt. Zipporah has no doubt listened to Moses relate how God called him to return to Egypt and deliver his fellow Hebrews from slavery. It is at an inn on the road that one of the strangest episodes in the entire book of Exodus occurs. In chapter 4 we are told that God seeks "to kill" Moses (4:24)—the very Moses whom he has just called to deliver Israel from the Egyptians. Such an action seems inexplicable at first, yet it is easier to understand as we analyze just what Moses's calling is and will be. He will lead the children of Israel out of slavery in the land of Egypt to Sinai, where they will enter into a covenant with their God to keep his laws. In fact, Moses will be known throughout history as the great lawgiver. If he is going to ask the children of Israel to keep God's laws, then he had better be an example of one who keeps them himself. In their haste to leave for Egypt, Moses has failed to circumcise his newborn son, Eliezer.

We might ask ourselves why Moses, who has already conversed with Yahweh at the burning bush, should be seized by such fear when he meets God at the inn. Rabbinic commentaries explain that Moses and

Zipporah have already retired for the night when God's glory concentrates itself in the tiny room and fills it near the point of rupture. Moses's previous experience with God occurred out in the open where he had been alone in reflection and God's glory had space to spread out. Here in the inn, Moses is overwhelmed by the intensity of God's presence. He has been involved with the routine activities of getting his family settled down for the night, and his mind has been on the mundane. He is not prepared for confronting God's power and glory and is overwhelmed by it, almost to the point of suffocation. The commentaries paint a picture of a dazed and numbed Moses who is overcome by a form of mental and physical paralysis. He is overwhelmed physically and is unable to function normally.[30]

Seeing all this, quick-witted Zipporah, the only person available to perform the rite, acts in the priestly role, seizes the flint, and circumcises her son. In order to transfer the effect of the rite to her husband, she touches the severed foreskin of her son to Moses's "feet," a common biblical euphemism for genitals.[31] After doing this she says, "Surely a bloody husband art thou to me" (Exodus 4:25). Or in other words, "a blood-bridegroom thou art to me." Zipporah calls Moses a "bridegroom of blood" because she has been compelled to acquire him anew as her husband through shedding her son's blood and conforming to the rite of circumcision. He is as good as dead to her, and she has to retrieve him from the dead and marry him again symbolically.

After the rite is complete, God retreats from Moses. She repeats the phrase, "A bloody husband thou art, because of the circumcision" (Exodus 4:26).[32] A Jewish commentator has interpreted this speech as being one made to her newborn son, saying, "With your blood, the blood of the [covenant], my bridegroom has been spared!"[33] Another scholar feels that this is Zipporah's way of getting in the "last word." After giving her husband back to God, she declares her relationship to Moses in a kind of symbolic naming: "You are truly a bridegroom of blood to me."[34] Kunin, a scholar who has examined reversals in Exodus, says that when Zipporah makes this statement, she "in effect, takes Moses as a husband, a reversal of the usual pattern where a husband takes a wife."[35] She is truly a woman ahead of her time. Another rabbinic commentator adds that Zipporah realizes in a flash of revelation that she must be the one to act in lieu of her incapacitated husband,[36] and the Talmud affirms that a woman may perform a circumcision if there is no male who is able to do so.[37]

The Targum of Exodus relates the tale in a similar fashion, with a slight variation on Zipporah's speech. After she circumcises her son, she approaches the Lord and says "On account of the blood of this circumcision let my husband be given (back) to me. And when [the Lord] had desisted from [Moses] she said, But for the blood of this circumcision my husband would have been condemned to die."[38]

It is irrefutable that Zipporah's decisive action saves the life of her husband. Moses is continually rescued by the women in his life. First, by the midwives, Shiphrah and Puah, who refuse to be dominated by the edict of the Pharaoh. Then, by his mother, who shrewdly obeys the mandate of the king by throwing her son into the river but only does so after placing him in a reed basket. Next, his sister, Miriam, deftly carries out an ingenious plan whereby Moses can be nursed by his own mother and get paid for it as well. The daughter of Pharaoh, moved with compassion for a condemned child, rescues the baby from certain death and gives him a privileged childhood complete with the benefits of a royal education. And finally, Zipporah saves him by performing a religious ritual in his behalf. Did all these women in Moses's life fulfill their divine birthright as *ezers*? Clearly they were all strong. They were all rescuers. Without their intervention in delivering Moses from death on numerous occasions, there would not have been a prophet to deliver the children of Israel from bondage.

Notes

1. Shera Aranoff Tuchman and Sandra E. Rapoport, *Moses' Women* (Jersey City: KTAV Publishing House, 2008), 21.

2. Rashi in Tuchman and Rapoport, *Moses' Women*, 22.

3. Sh'mot Rabbah in Tuchman and Rapoport, *Moses' Women*, 23.

4. Ibid., 24.

5. Rashi in Tuchman and Rapoport, *Moses' Women*, 39–40.

6. Sh'mot Rabbah in Tuchman and Rapoport, *Moses' Women*, 40.

7. Pirkei d'Rabi Eliezer in Tuchman and Rapoport, *Moses' Women*, 49

8. Sh'mot in Tuchman and Rapoport, *Moses' Women*, 52.

9. Flavius Josephus, Antiquities of the Jews in *The Complete Works of Josephus*. Translated by William Whiston. (Grand Rapids: Kregel Publications, 1974), 56.

10. Alschich, Rabbeinu Bachya, Chizkuni, and Ibn Ezra in Tuchman and Rapoport, *Moses' Women*, 53–54.

11. Netziv in Tuchman and Rapoport, *Moses' Women*, 57.

12. Sha'arei Aharon, Pirkei d'Rabi Eliezer, Sh'mot Rabbah, the Malbin in Tuchman and Rapoport, 59–61.

13. The Rav and Pirkei d'Rabi Eliezer in Tuchman and Rapoport, *Moses' Women*, 62–63.

14. Torat HaChidah in Tuchman and Rapoport, *Moses' Women*, 64.

15. Rashbam and the Netziv in Tuchman and Rapoport, *Moses' Women*, 68–69.

16. Alschich in Tuchman and Rapoport, *Moses' Women*, 69–70.

17. Aggadot Yam HaTalmud in Tuchman and Rapoport, *Moses' Women*, 70.

18. See Deuteronomy 18:15 and Acts 3:22.

19. The Malbim and Abarbanel in Tuchman and Rapoport, *Moses' Women*, 71–72.

20. The Malbim and the Netziv in Tuchman and Rapoport, *Moses' Women*, 72–75.

21. Elie Wiesel, *Wise Men and Their Tales* (New York: Schocken Books, 2003), 57.

22. The Malbim and the Rav in Tuchman and Rapoport, *Moses' Women*, 81–82.

23. Ibn Ezra, Torat HaChidah, and the Malbim in Tuchman and Rapoport, *Moses' Women*, 82.

24. Sh'mot Rabbah in Tuchman and Rapoport, *Moses' Women*, 85.

25. Sforno and Ibn Ezra in Tuchman and Rapoport, *Moses' Women*, 86.

26. Sh'mot Rabbah in Tuchman and Rapoport, *Moses' Women*, 100.

27. Ha'Ma'or Shebatorah, Rashi, Sforno, the Talmid (Nedarim 65) and Sh'mot Rabbah(1:32) in Tuchman and Rapoport, *Moses' Women*, 102–103.

28. Megan McKenna, *Leave Her Alone* (Maryknoll: Orbis Books, 2000), 175.

29. The Ramban in Tuchman and Rapoport, *Moses' Women*, 124.

30. Abarbanel in Tuchman and Rapoport, *Moses' Women*, 132–33.

31. *The Women's Bible Commentary*. Edited by Carol A. Newsom and Sharon H. Ringe. (Louisville: Westminster/John Knox Press, 1992), 31.

32. C. K. Keil, and F. Delitzsch, *Commentary on the Old Testament in Ten Volumes, Volume I, The Pentateuch: Three Volumes in One* (Grand Rapids: William B. Erdmans Publishing, 1991), 460.

33. Sh'mot Rabba in Tuchman and Rapoport, *Moses' Women*, 137.

34. Christine Benvenuto, "Envisioning Zipporah" in *Tikkun*, 13.4, 62.

35. Seth D. Kunin, "The Bridegroom of Blood: a Structuralist Analysis," in *Journal for the Study of the Old Testament* (1996), 13.

36. Chizkuni in Tuchman and Rapoport, *Moses' Women*, 135.

37. The Talmud in Tuchman and Rapoport, *Moses' Women*, 135.

38. J. W. Etheridge, *The Targums of Onkelos and Jonathan ben Uzziel on the Pentateuch* (London: Longman, Green, Longman, Roberts, and Green, 1865), 353.

CHAPTER 8

Deborah and Jael: "Into the Hand of a Woman"
Judges 4–5

DEBORAH IS UNIQUE AMONG OLD Testament figures. No one else possesses such a distinct combination of leadership qualities. Deborah is a military leader, a mother in Israel, a prophetess, a poetess, and even a judge. She is the ultimate multitasker and supermom. As a prophetess, she sees the hand of God in all events, relationships, and conditions. As a woman of insight, her words are followed without question. The people of Israel come to her for legal counsel and leadership in a time when "there was no king in Israel: every man did that which was right in his own eyes" (Judges 21:25).

In his version of the story in the pseudepigrapha, Pseudo-Philo elaborates on the theme of this crisis of leadership. In *Biblical Antiquities*, he says, "The sons of Israel did not have anyone to appoint for themselves as judge" (30:1). Because they do not have anyone to lead them in heeding God's commandments and statutes, they suffer the consequences of their disobedience—the loss of God's protection from oppression by their enemies. Therefore, "the children of Israel again did evil in the sight of the Lord" (Judges 4:1). Pseudo-Philo expands this statement to say, "their heart fell away, and they forgot the promise and transgressed the ways that Moses and Joshua . . . had commanded them, and they were led astray after the daughters of the Amorites and served their gods" (30:1). It seems you just can't leave children unattended for long periods of time.

God responds to their betrayal with anger, but then he provides the people a chance to reclaim their covenant relationship with him. Pseudo-Philo's narrative includes the dramatic appearance of an angel to the people to communicate this message. The angel says that because of their transgressions, God "will arouse their enemies, and they will rule over them. And then all the people will say, 'Because we have transgressed the ways of God and of our fathers, on account of this these things have come upon us' " (30:2). After this announcement, the angel makes a pledge to send them a leader who will "rule" over them and "enlighten" them for forty years—and the leader is to be a *woman*! Being a ruler or teacher was extremely unconventional for a Jewish woman in the ancient Near East. In *The Legends of the Jews*, Louis Ginzberg renders this line as "Then I will send a woman unto them, and she will shine for them as a light for forty years."[1]

Another Jewish legend holds that Deborah's husband has not been schooled in Torah. His wife tells him, "Come, I will make wicks for you; take them to the Holy Place in Shiloh. Your portion will then be with men of worth in Israel [who will be studying by the light of your wicks], and you will be worthy of life in the world-to-come."[2] He carries lamps into the sanctuary where he is called Lapidoth, or "Flames." Deborah makes the wicks for these oil lamps very thick so that they burn a long time. Therefore, God glorifies her saying, "Thou takest pains to shed light in My house, and I will let thy light, thy fame, shine abroad in the whole land."[3]

Bible scholar Cheryl Brown asserts that Pseudo-Philo describes Deborah as one who "enlightens" on at least two levels. First, Pseudo-Philo interprets *ešeth lapidoth*—translated in the King James Version of Judges 4:4 as "wife of Lapidoth"—in a literal way. The Hebrew word *ešeth* can mean both "woman" or "wife," and *lapidoth* means "torches" or can perhaps be a proper name. Since her husband is also known as Lapidoth, this may just be a way to identify Deborah as his wife, but

Pseudo-Philo clearly interprets it to mean Deborah is a "woman of fire" or "light," who will "enlighten" the people. Secondly, Pseudo-Philo associates Deborah with Moses, whom he also portrays as "enlightening" the people (11:2). God directed Moses to deliver his law to the children of Israel, and now a woman, Deborah, will "enlighten them for forty years" (30:2). "Like Moses," Brown concludes, "Deborah calls Israel to observe the Torah, leads them in their miraculous deliverance, and shepherds them for forty years."[4]

The text of *Biblical Antiquities* is similar to Judges 4:2 in describing the Lord's punishment of his wayward people: "And after this the Lord aroused against them Jabin the king of Hazor, and he began to attack them. And he had Sisera as the commander of his army, who had eight thousand iron chariots . . . . And Israel feared him very much, and the people could not resist all the days of Sisera" (30:3). In the Judges account, Sisera only has nine hundred chariots, but the number is still formidable because the Israelites have none.

Ginzberg recorded that Jewish tradition passed on many legends about Sisera's prowess:

> When he was thirty years old, he had conquered the whole world. At the sound of his voice the strongest of walls fell in a heap, and the wild animals in the woods were chained to the spot by fear. The proportions of his body were vast beyond description. If he took a bath in the river, and dived beneath the surface, enough fish were caught in his beard to feed a multitude, and it required no less than nine hundred horses to draw the chariot in which he rode.[e]

Pseudo-Philo expands the Bible's terse "And the children of Israel cried unto the Lord" (Judges 4:3) into a stirring scene of contrition. After the sons of Israel have been badly humiliated they gather together to the mountain of Judah and lament:

> We say that we are more blessed than other nations, and behold now we have been humiliated more than all peoples so that we cannot dwell in our own land and our enemies have power over us. And now who has done all these things to us? Is it not our own wicked deeds, because we have forsaken the Lord of our fathers and have walked in these ways that have not profited us? And now come, let us fast for seven days . . . . And who knows perhaps God will be reconciled with his inheritance so as not to destroy the plant of his vineyard. (30:4)

Unlike Judges 4:6–7, where the people gather to prepare for combat, the purpose of this gathering is to fast and pray for deliverance. The repentance of the people is an important precursor to their liberation. The author seems to want to emphasize that Israel is engaged in more than a military battle. They must win the spiritual battle before they can begin the military one.

Pseudo-Philo has created a great sense of anticipation in these initial scenes of his narrative, just as the movie trailers of today seek to do. The people *want* to believe in God's promised deliverer, but they don't know who she will be or when she will come. Deborah is introduced only after this suspense has time to build. Judges 4:3–4 implies simply that the Lord sends Deborah as a result of the people crying to the Lord. Pseudo-Philo elevates Deborah's importance to the people by relating their pleas in more detail: "When the people had fasted seven days and sat in sackcloth, the Lord sent to them on the seventh day Deborah" (30:5).

Deborah establishes in her first dealings with the Israelites that she has been called to do more than bring political deliverance. She acts as a prophetess, first speaking words of reproof to the people and comparing them to a sheep that is about to be slaughtered. Both the sheep (Israel) and the slaughterer (God) are silent, even though the slaughterer is sorrowful over what he must do. She then tells Israel that they are like a flock that the Lord has carefully shepherded and blessed—the Lord has given them the Law to protect them and prophets to correct them. He has "commanded the luminaries" and "they stood still in their assigned places." She says that "when your enemies came against you, [God] rained down hailstones on them and destroyed them. And Moses and Joshua . . . commanded you, and you did not obey them" (30:5). She compares them to iron, which is pliant while in the flame (or when chastened) but "reverts to its original hardness" when it is removed from the fire, thus implying that the people are obedient to their leader while he is among them but quickly turn from their righteousness after his death. She even predicts, "after my departure you will start sinning again" (30:7). This calls to mind the last speech of Moses when he prophesies the fall of the people into apostasy: "For I know that after my death ye will utterly corrupt yourselves, and turn aside from the way which I have commanded you" (Deuteronomy

31:29). Again, the similarity of these two phrases is another example of Deborah's association with Moses, and it elevates her as his female counterpart.[6]

After Deborah predicts that the people will sin after her death, she offers them words of hope: "And behold now the Lord will take pity on you today, not because of you but because of his covenant that he established with your fathers and the oath that he has sworn not to abandon you forever" (30:7). Her declaration—"Our fathers are dead, but the God who established the covenant with them is life"—mimics Deuteronomy 30:20: "For [the Lord] is thy life."[7]

In recounting the story of the liberation of Israel from Jabin, king of the Canaanites, Pseudo-Philo adheres to the biblical account quite closely, but he still fashions the narrative to emphasize the points he wishes to make. In Judges 4:6, Deborah orders Barak,[8] the general of Israel's armies, to ready his forces and prepare for battle, but he hesitates. His reply to her is quite astounding, considering the times and the culture of the Israelites. He says, "If thou wilt go with me, then I will go: but if thou wilt not go with me, then I will not go" (Judges 4:8). Deborah answers, in effect, "I will go with you, but if you do it that way, the honor of the victory will not be yours, for the Lord 'shall sell Sisera into the hand of a woman'" (see Judges 4:9).[9]

In *Biblical Antiquities,* Pseudo-Philo fairly accurately depicts the essence of Judges 4:6, in which Deborah calls Barak to prepare for battle, but then he omits Barak's refusal to go unless accompanied by Deborah as well as her ensuing censure. He moves the prediction that Sisera will be delivered into the hand of a woman into another setting in order to emphasize different points.

Ginzberg explains why the challenge given to Deborah and Barak to lead the attack was no small task. "It is comparable with nothing less than Joshua's undertaking to conquer Canaan. Joshua had triumphed over only thirty-one of the sixty-two kings of Palestine, leaving at large as many as he had subdued. Under the leadership of Sisera these thirty-one unconquered kings opposed Israel."[10]

In *Biblical Antiquities,* Deborah next speaks lines that give the amazing victory over Sisera's forces almost cosmic proportions. She prophesies, "I see the stars moved from their course and ready for battle on your side. Also I see the lightning that cannot be moved from its course going forth to hinder the works of the chariots of those who glory in the might of Sisera" (31:1). The thunderstorm is not just a fortuitous event that aids the Israelites in winning the battle over their assailants, but the stars and the lightning are personified and enter the conflict as characters that enable Israel to prevail. The story continues,

> And when Deborah and the people and Barak went down to meet the enemies, immediately the Lord disturbed the movement of his stars. And he said to them, "Hurry and go, for your enemies fall upon you; and confound their arms and crush the power of their heart, because I have come that my people may prevail. For even if my people have sinned, nevertheless I will have mercy on them." (31:2)

Before the battle begins, Deborah presents the three things Sisera has boasted he will do and contrasts them with the three ways he will be punished. He has boasted that he will come down and attack Israel with his mighty arm, and she counters with the prediction that "the arm of a weak woman [will] attack him." He has boasted that he will divide their spoils among his servants, when—in actuality—"maidens [will] take *his* spoils." He has bragged that he will take for himself many beautiful women as concubines, but she prophesies, "even he [will] fall into the hands of a woman" (31:1). This plot has potential for a good made-for-TV movie, don't you think?

In the rest of the narrative, Pseudo-Philo emphasizes the fact that God can bring victory to the weak if he is on their side. He does not need might and power to triumph but only righteousness. He will fight battles *for* his people, if they are holy. Pseudo-Philo makes the comment that Sisera does not escape because of his own cunning, but only because it is divinely decreed. He records that the stars "did not destroy Sisera, because so it has been commanded them" (31:2).

In the Judges version of the story, Sisera lights down from his chariot and flees on his feet (Judges 4:15). Conversely, in the *Biblical Antiquities* account, Sisera flees the battle scene on horseback "to save his life" (31:3), displaying that even in flight, he is still a man of power. Pseudo-Philo does this to heighten his sense of paradox because although Sisera *seems* strong, appearances are sometimes deceiving.

Jael, the wife of his friend Heber the Kenite, comes out to meet him. Pseudo-Philo adds that Jael has "adorned herself" and is "very beautiful in appearance" (31:3). Jewish tradition adds that, besides wearing "rich garments and jewels," she is "unusually beautiful, and her voice was the most seductive ever a woman possessed."[11]

In the tradition of Judith, Jael uses the weapons she has in her arsenal in order to accomplish her desires. She is a beautiful woman. Sisera is exhausted and battle-weary. She tells him to take some food and rest until evening. She offers him respite, refreshment, and protection. As he approaches his resting place, he fantasizes that he will take this beautiful woman home to be his wife. When he sees roses scattered on the bed, he says, "If I am saved, I will go to my mother and Jael will be my wife" (31:3). He asks for water. She offers him milk, seeming to be the perfect host. But Sisera is really in Jael's power. Although he feels safe and secure, he is weak, and *she* is strong.

Pseudo-Philo adds an angle that is absent in the biblical account. In the Judges narrative, Jael acts only of her own accord. In *Biblical Antiquities*, Jael is portrayed as being divinely directed. While Sisera is sleeping, Jael goes out to the flock to get milk. As she milks she prays, saying:

> Did you not choose Israel alone and liken it to no animal except to the ram that goes before and leads the flock? And so look and see that Sisera has made a plan and said, 'I will go and punish the flock of the Most Powerful One.' And I will take from the milk of these animals to which you have likened your people, and I will go and give him to drink. And when he will have drunk, he will be off guard, and afterward I will kill him. (31:5)

We do not know if Sisera will be off guard because he is sexually aroused, courtesy of the beautifully adorned Jael, or because the warm milk has had a soporific effect on him. As she milks and prays, she expresses her inner musing to God. "But this will be the sign that you act along with me, Lord, that, when I enter while Sisera is asleep, he will rise up and ask me again and again, saying, 'Give me water to drink,' then I know that my prayer has been heard" (31:5). She knows that the Lord has destined Israel to be the eminent nation in the world, yet she finds herself enslaved to Sisera and Jabin, the Canaanite king.

She decides to become an instrument in the hands of God to overthrow this tyrant who has been delivered into her hands. She pleads for a sign from God to give her assurance that he sanctions her actions. Although she is a "weak" woman, with the Lord's help she can bring down the mighty Sisera.

When Jael returns to the tent, Sisera wakes up and asks for the milk. Jael takes wine, mixes it with the milk, and gives it to Sisera. He drinks and falls asleep, and Jael takes a stake in her left hand and approaches him, saying, "If God will work this sign with me, I know that Sisera will fall into my hands. Behold, I will throw him down on the ground from the bed on which he sleeps; and if he does not feel it, I know that he has been handed over" (31:7). She pushes Sisera onto the ground from the bed, but he is too groggy to feel it. Jael again prays, "Strengthen in me today, Lord, my arm on account of you and your people and those who hope in you" (31:7).

Jael then takes the stake, puts it on his temple, and strikes it with a wooden hammer. As he is dying, Sisera has strength enough to utter his last words: "Behold pain has taken hold of me, Jael, and I die like a woman." Jael wishes to emphasize the demeaning nature of his death and adds, "Go, boast before your father in hell and tell him that you have fallen into the hands of a woman" (31:7). In the King James Version of the song of Deborah in Judges, Deborah praises Jael saying, "Blessed above women shall Jael the wife of Heber the Kenite be, blessed shall she be above women in the tent" (Judges 5:24). One additional grisly detail is provided in this account: "She put her hand to the nail, and her right hand to the workmen's hammer; and with the hammer she smote Sisera, she smote off his head, when she had pierced and stricken through his temples" (Judges 5:26). I can imagine the strength it would take to drive a tent stake through a man's skull. Just to make sure the deed is done completely, she cuts his head off. In the New International Version of the verse she "crushes" his head. She must have really been motivated to go to all that extra effort. The Hebrew text literally says, "between her feet he bowed." Does he attempt to raise his headless body and "bow" as he is dying? I guess we'll have to wait and see the movie.

Barak soon arrives on the scene, very disappointed that he has not found Sisera. Jael goes out to meet him and invites him in, saying,

"Come, enter in, . . . and I will hand over to you your enemy whom you pursued but did not find." Barak, seeing Sisera dead, says, "Blessed be the Lord, who sent his spirit and said, 'Into the hand of a woman Sisera will be handed over'" (31:9).

The song of Deborah continues with a taunt. Deborah envisions Sisera's mother anxiously awaiting his return from battle. When he is slow in returning, she speculates as to the cause of his tardiness: "The mother of Sisera looked out at a window, and cried through the lattice, Why is his chariot so long in coming? why tarry the wheels of his chariots?" (Judges 5:28). She conjectures that they have been so successful in battle that dividing up the spoils of war is taking longer than necessary. "Have they not sped? have they not divided the prey; to every man a damsel or two; to Sisera a prey of divers colours, a prey of divers colours of needlework, of divers colours of needlework on both sides, meet for the necks of them that take the spoil?" (Judges 5:30). It is impossible to miss the irony of this statement. Yes, Sisera has indeed encountered a damsel, and he has perished at her hands. Sisera's mother pictures the beautiful needlework that her son will take as spoil after the battle and how wonderful it will look adorning his victorious neck. Little does she know that his neck is missing its head because it has encountered Jael with something larger than a needle in her hands. The "needle" that she wields is a tent stake that leaves Sisera very unlike the picture of the victorious warrior his mother envisions.

It is hard to miss the point that Pseudo-Philo hammers home through the words of all the major characters—the angel, Deborah, Jael, Sisera, and Barak: A weak woman can defeat the mightiest warrior. Those who boast in their own strength, although they may appear powerful, are not as strong as those who, in their weakness, trust in God to bring about victory. At the time that Pseudo-Philo wrote in the first century, the Jewish people had lost hope of ever being able to return to their native land again, having seen Jerusalem and their beloved temple destroyed. He wants them to know that God can strengthen them to overcome their enemies.

In her book, *Leave Her Alone*, Megan McKenna points out two notable ironies in this episode. First, the battle is won by nature itself, so that the Israelites do not even have to fight the enemy in order to defeat them. In addition to the lightning and the fire, there is a flash flood at the Kishon River, which mires all of Sisera's chariots and renders them useless. Second, Sisera is defeated by the wife of an ally—a *woman*. All his might and prowess and reputation have come to naught because the God of Israel is not with him.[12]

After this miraculous deliverance, Deborah, Barak, and all the people sing a hymn. This draws another parallel to Moses, who sang a hymn to the Lord with Miriam after he delivered the children of Israel from the hands of the Egyptians at the Red Sea (see Exodus 15:1). However, in this story the distinct leader is a woman. Deborah is clearly in Moses's place. The hymn chronicles the mighty works of God among the patriarchs, beginning with the delivery of Abraham from the fire, as well as the delivery of his son Isaac from being sacrificed (32:1–4). It describes the children of Jacob and their sojourn in Egypt, and their delivery from the hands of their wicked taskmasters there. It speaks of the establishment of the covenant with Israel at Mount Sinai, with Moses as God's "beloved witness" (32:8). It tells of Moses's vision of the future of Israel and Joshua's victory over the Canaanites (32:9–10). Finally, it describes Deborah's victory over the forces of Sisera, although the only name mentioned specifically is Jael's. "Jael is glorified among women, because she alone has made straight the way to success by killing Sisera with her own hands" (32:12). The message of the hymn is clear—"[God] has remembered both his recent and ancient promises and shown his saving power to us" (32:12).

Deborah entreats all the hosts of heaven to tell these ancient fathers in the resting place of souls that await judgment day that "the Most Powerful has not forgotten the least of the promises that he established with us saying, 'Many wonders will I do for your sons'" (32:13). This promise alludes back to the encouragement Deborah gave to the people when she was first sent to them: "The Lord will work wonders among you and hand over your enemies into your hands" (30:7). At that time, she said that God would do this "because of the covenant that he established with your fathers" (30:7). Deborah testifies to Israel that God is faithful to his covenant promises. She speaks of the stars fighting for Israel because they had been so commanded by God. Just as God had marshaled the stars to fight against Sisera's armies, so would he come to their aid in the future: "If Israel falls into distress, it will call upon those witnesses along with these servants [the stars], and they will form a delegation to the Most High, and he will remember that day and send the saving power of his covenant" (32:14). After Deborah has finished speaking, she and the people go to Shiloh and offer sacrifices to the Lord. Pseudo-Philo concludes by saying, "And Deborah came down from there and judged Israel forty years" (32:18).

The New International Version of Judges 4:5 records that "she held court under the Palm of Deborah between Ramah and Bethel in the hill country of Ephraim, and the Israelites came to her to have their disputes decided."[13] Ginzberg discloses that "she dispensed judgment in the open air, for it was not becoming that men should visit a woman in her house."[14]

As her final days draw near, Deborah gathers the people together and says to them, "Listen now my people. Behold I am warning you as a woman of God and am enlightening you as one from the female race; and obey me like a mother and heed my words" (33:1). Think of this speech the next time you or someone you know says, "Because I'm the mom, that's why."

Pseudo-Philo accentuates Deborah's role as a mother, which perhaps indicates that he regards her role as a mother and her role as a judge and prophet to be equally important. According to Leila Leah Bronner, "her prominence stemmed not only from her role as prophet and judge, but also from her role as mother."[15] Pseudo-Philo would no doubt subscribe to the aphorism, "The hand that rocks the cradle rules the world."

As Deborah is speaking her final words to the people, exhorting them to "make straight [their] ways," they raise their voices together and weep, saying, "Behold now, Mother, you die, and to whom do you commend your sons whom you are leaving? Pray therefore for us, and after your departure your soul will be mindful of us forever" (33:4). The people are concerned about who will lead them when she is gone and who would enlighten them in the future. The level to which her people will miss her makes one thing very clear—Deborah has been of such eminence and has had such a powerful influence on the people that no one can truly replace her.

Pseudo-Philo records similar feelings and concerns of Moses's people when Moses bids them farewell: "Who will give us another shepherd like Moses or such a judge for the sons of Israel to pray always for our sins and to be heard for our iniquities?" (19:3). The words "judge" and "shepherd" are used synonymously in *Biblical Antiquities* and both act chiefly as mediators, which function is vastly different from the way the word "judge" is used in Judges, where a "judge" is fundamentally a liberator. According to Pseudo-Philo, Deborah and Moses are counterparts, both fulfilling the masculine *and* feminine roles of leading, delivering, encouraging, teaching, and shepherding.[16]

Deborah dies. The people bury her in the city of her fathers, and, astoundingly, they mourn for her seventy days. It was customary to mourn for a person for no more than thirty days, although the patriarch Jacob was mourned for seventy days (Genesis 50:3).[17] No doubt, this extended period of mourning demonstrated the extent to which Deborah's people esteemed and loved her. The people sing this lament:

> Behold there has perished a mother from Israel,
> and the holy one who exercised leadership in the house of Jacob.
> She firmed up the fence about her generation,
> and her generation will grieve over her. (33:6)

The first statement, that Deborah is a "mother from Israel," bespeaks the qualities of nurturing, admonishing, instructing, guiding, and protecting that are a part of this all-important role. She is called a "holy one," a title reserved for those with special spiritual acuity and piety—those who work miracles, have visions, or stand as mediators between the people and God. She is called a "leader in the house of Jacob," assuredly fulfilling the angel's prediction that "a woman [would] rule over them and enlighten them for forty years" (30:2). Lastly, she has "firmed up the fence about her generation." Perhaps this sentiment comes from the Judges 5 account, which describes the civilization that existed before Deborah started to rule over the people. People were afraid to travel on the highways, and travelers "walked through byways" (Judges 5:6). They lived scattered about the country without the protection of fences or walls around their environs. This statement may depict that former lawlessness and anarchy. Or perhaps the word "fence" could be interpreted more metaphorically, referring to the law of Moses that keeps the Israelites separate from their Canaanite neighbors and keeps them from being defiled by other gods.[18]

There are many reasons why Deborah stands out as a unique figure in the history of Israel. She provides "enlightened" leadership in a time when direction is scarce. God delivers the children of Israel "into the hand of a woman" because no strong male leader is present. If an *ezer* means being strong, then she indisputably fulfills her role as an *ezer*. She has the strength of a man in guiding Israel and helping the people resolve their disputes. She has the wisdom to be sought out for her "enlightenment." She sees the hand of God in all things, both great and small, and sings praises to him for his mighty works. If an *ezer* means being a savior, then Deborah is the quintessential *ezer*. She inspires strength in Barak to lead his ten thousand men against the forces of Sisera. Her support enables him to believe he can obey the call of the Lord and emerge victorious. Without her, the Israelites would not have been delivered from the oppression of the king of the Canaanites. The Lord works through her to inspire the people to repent so that he can manifest his power in rescuing them from their enemies. There cannot be a doubt in their minds that he is fighting their battles for them. Deborah sings the Lord's praises and assures the Israelites that—just as he kept his covenant with their fathers in the past and delivered them from their enemies—so too will he uphold the covenant with them in the future if they will only trust in him.

Notes

1. Louis Ginzberg, *The Legends of the Jews*, vol. 4. (Baltimore: Johns Hopkins University Press, 1913, 1941), 35.

2. Megan McKenna, *Leave Her Alone* (Maryknoll: Orbis Books, 2000), 143.

3. Ibid.

4. Cheryl Anne Brown, *No Longer Be Silent: First Century Jewish Portraits of Biblical Women* (Louisville: Westminster/John Knox Press, 1992), 43–44.

5. Ginzberg, *The Legends of the Jews*, 35.

6. Brown, *No Longer Be Silent: First Century Jewish Portraits of Biblical Women*, 49

7. Ibid., 48–49.

8. Jewish tradition held that Barak was Deborah's husband. See Ginzberg, *The Legends of the Jews*, 35.

9. McKenna, *Leave Her Alone*, 141.

10. Ginzberg, *The Legends of the Jews*, 36.

11. Ibid., 37.

12. McKenna, *Leave Her Alone*, 141.

13. *The Holy Bible*, New International Version (Grand Rapids, Michigan: Zondervan Bible Publishers, 1984).

14. Ginzberg, *The Legends of the Jews*, 35–36.

15. Leila Leah Bronner, *Stories of Biblical Mothers: Maternal Power in the Hebrew Bible* (Lanham: University Press of America, 2004), 81.

16. Brown, *No Longer Be Silent: First Century Jewish Portraits of Biblical Women*, 68–69.

17. Ibid., 69.

18. Ibid., 69–71; and McKenna, *Leave Her Alone*, 145.

CHAPTER 9

Hannah: Silent No Longer
1 Samuel 1–2, Biblical Antiquities

HANNAH'S STORY IS ONE OF quiet catastrophe—the catastrophe of empty arms, the oft-repeated and almost stereotypical catastrophe of barrenness and infertility. It is not a catastrophe on the same scale as the destruction of the temple or the capture of the ark of the covenant, but, to Hannah, childlessness is calamity.[1] And to make matters worse, her husband's second wife, Peninnah, maliciously throws salt on Hannah's raw wound. Despite these trials, Hannah is portrayed as an intensely devout woman who trusts in God despite the scorn from her rival and the lack of support from those closest to her.

The book of *Biblical Antiquities* in the *Old Testament Pseudepigrapha* adds many details to the story of Hannah. Here, the author Pseudo-Philo reworks the elements of the biblical narrative so that Hannah's character is enhanced and she emerges as a heroine separate from her celebrated prophet-son Samuel.

In chapter 48 of *Biblical Antiquities*, Pseudo-Philo writes that there is a leadership crisis in the Israelite community: "They had no leader in those days, and each one did what was pleasing in his own eyes" (48:4, see also Judges 17:6). The people recognize this as a great problem and petition God to help them find a leader: "And in that time the sons of Israel began to make a request from the Lord, and they said, 'Let us all cast lots to see who it is who can rule us as Kenaz did. For perhaps we will find a man who may free us from our distress, for it is not appropriate for the people to be without a ruler'" (49:1).

Kenaz is a figure invented by Pseudo-Philo who has been the people's prophet and defender of the covenant. They follow the precedent of casting lots to determine who the new leader is to be, just as Kenaz was chosen after the death of Joshua in *Biblical Antiquities* 25. Thankfully, there are no "hanging chads" to worry about when casting lots. The casting of lots is a device the people use to ascertain knowledge by mystical means. This time, however, when the lots do not point to any leader, the people interpret it as a sign that they are "not worthy to be heard by the Lord" (49:2). The people grow desperate.

They cast lots again, this time by tribe, and when no particular tribe is designated, they again take it as a sign "that God has hated his people and his soul has detested us" (49:2). A man named Nethez encourages the hopeless people to repent, and they beseech God again—this time casting lots by cities. Everyone eagerly awaits the revelation of who the new leader is to be. The lot falls on the city Ramathaim, and the people rejoice that God has acknowledged them. Lots are again cast to determine the appointed leader, but when the lot falls upon Elkanah, he refuses to accept the responsibility. They continue the discussion with God who finally says, "His son who will be born from him, he will rule among you and prophesy. And from this time on, a ruler will not be lacking from you for many years" (49:7). The people respond, "Behold, Lord, Elkanah has ten sons, and who of them will rule or prophesy?" (49:8).

God's reply introduces the predicament described in the biblical narrative of 1 Samuel 1—that Elkanah has two wives, one has children and one does not. He mentions the one with children by name: "None of the sons of Peninnah can rule the people, but the one who is born from the sterile woman whom I have given to him as a wife will be a prophet before me. And I will love him as I have loved Isaac, and his name will be before me always" (49:8). God apparently loves drama, for he has once again chosen to designate a prophet born of a sterile woman. Both Isaac and Samuel are cherished because they are born to barren women.

Through the use of such suspense-heightening literary devices as the casting of lots, Pseudo-Philo has placed the birth of the prophet Samuel in a much larger context. Samuel is not just the answer to a barren woman's prayer for a son, he is the answer to an entire nation's prayers for a leader. Now, Elkanah fades from the spotlight, and the still-unnamed Hannah emerges as the one who will be God's instrument in fulfilling his pledge to a nation by giving birth to a prophet.

Pseudo-Philo reworks the biblical narrative in order to emphasize Hannah's strength of character. While 1 Samuel 1:2 simply states the fact that Elkanah had two wives and that Peninnah had children but Hannah had no children, Pseudo-Philo elaborates on the rivalry between Peninnah and Hannah: "And Elkanah had two wives. The name of one was Hannah, and the name of the other was Peninnah. And because Peninnah had sons and Hannah did not, Peninnah taunted her" (50:1). A fertile second wife taunting a barren first wife draws upon the pattern of Hagar and Sarah and also upon the rivalry between Leah and Rachel.[2] Leah, Hagar, and Peninnah are fertile, yet they do not enjoy the love and favor from their husbands that they seek. Peninnah's bitterness is not brought out in the biblical narrative until 1 Samuel 1:7. In 1 Samuel, Peninnah torments Hannah on the journey to the yearly sacrifice at Shiloh. *Biblical Antiquities* expands our view of this abuse and reveals the torture that Hannah must endure *daily* at home.

Peninnah ridicules Hannah by saying, " 'What does it profit you that Elkanah your husband loves you, for you are a dry tree? And I know that my husband will love me, because he delights in the sight of my sons standing around him like a plantation of olive trees.' And so it was when she was taunting her daily, and Hannah was saddened very much" (50:1–2). The "dry tree" image that Peninnah employs brings to mind Isaiah 56:3, in which a eunuch laments that he does not have an inheritance in Israel. The Lord tells him, "The eunuchs that keep my sabbaths, and choose the things that please me, and take hold of my covenant; even unto them will I give in mine house and within my walls a place and a name better than of sons and of daughters: I will give them an everlasting name, that shall not be cut off" (Isaiah 56:4–5). This citation from Isaiah declares that "a place and a name" in the house of the Lord will be the reward of righteous living, *not* physical offspring. Hannah echoes this sentiment when she declares, "I know that neither she that has many sons is rich nor she who has few is poor, but whoever abounds in the will of God is rich" (50:5). A woman's ability to bear offspring does not indicate her spirituality and worth.

Pseudo-Philo tells us that Hannah's barrenness is not a result of sin, because "Hannah [has] been fearing God from her youth" (50:2). She possesses the spiritual confidence that comes from righteous living. She tells God, "I have walked before you from the day of my youth" (50:4). God has ordained Hannah's infertility for a divine purpose. He will permit her barrenness in order to work a greater miracle among the children of Israel, but she is not yet aware of it because "Eli the priest [does] not want to tell her that a prophet [has] been foreordained to be born from her" (50:8).[3]

In the next section of the pseudepigraphical account, the family makes its journey to Shiloh for Passover. It is about fifteen miles from their home in Ramah to Shiloh.[4] Elkanah goes to offer the sacrifice while the women remain at their place of lodging. He returns to find Hannah miserable and dejected because of Peninnah's taunting. Hannah does not return Peninnah's taunts with hostility but merely retreats within herself, isolating herself from the feast following the sacrifice and hiding in her grief. After we discover what Peninnah has said to Hannah, we understand the reason for her weeping and loss of appetite:

> A wife is not really loved even if her husband loves her or her beauty. Let Hannah not boast in her appearance; but she who boasts, let her boast when she sees her offspring before her. And when among women the fruit of her womb is not so, love will be in vain. For what did it profit Rachel that Jacob loved her? And unless the fruit of her womb had been given to him, his love would have been in vain. (50:2)

Although Peninnah attests that her joy is full because of her offspring, it is almost as if "the lady doth protest too much,"[5] and she sounds as if she is trying to convince herself of her happiness. Although she would have others believe that her ability to reproduce has brought her a sense of self-worth, her words betray that she has not received the joy and fulfillment that she claims, and that Elkanah's unabashed love for Hannah is a rock in her shoe.

The Bible relates that Elkanah discerns Hannah's distress and says to her, "Hannah, why weepest thou? and why eatest thou not? and why is thy heart grieved? am not I better to thee than ten sons?" (1 Samuel 1:8). Under the circumstances, who wouldn't lose her appetite from being tormented constantly and having her barrenness paraded publicly? Her despondency is certainly understandable.

Trevor Dennis explains Elkanah's comment in greater detail. Elkanah may have good intentions, Dennis explains, but *he* is not childless and cannot understand the depth of Hannah's pain. He understands things from a different perspective. He apparently thinks that his love for Hannah is enough to make up for her lack of children, but he is shortsighted. He asks her, "You have me—isn't that better than having ten sons?" He undoubtedly has good intentions, but this insensitive comment may just reinforce Hannah's loneliness. "Elkanah," Dennis writes, ". . . cannot through his own tenderness or passion satisfy her longing for a child, nor give her the status within the family . . . or the position in the community at large that such a child would bring. His suggestion that his love could compensate for all that is arrogant. It reveals he thinks he should be regarded as the centre of her world."[6]

Instead of validating her struggle, Elkanah tries to point out why Hannah should not be depressed. His "look on the bright side" attitude, as Carolyn Curtis James describes it, discounts her feelings, which are clearly very real and challenging for her. Although he gives Hannah the "worthy portion"[7] of the food at the annual feast to show her how much he loves her, her pain is still acute. *He* is not childless. For him, barrenness is a thing of the past. He has moved on and he wants Hannah to move on as well. But she cannot.[8]

The text of *Biblical Antiquities* is similar to the biblical account just cited, but here Elkanah praises Hannah in an intriguing way: "And when Hannah heard those words, her soul grew faint and poured out tears. And her husband saw her and said, 'Why are you sad? And why do you not eat? And why does your heart fall within you? Are not your ways of behaving better than the ten sons of Peninnah?' " (50:3).

With this passage, Pseudo-Philo shifts the focus from Elkanah's compassionate love for Hannah to Hannah's sterling character. Her "ways of behaving [are] better than the ten sons of Peninnah." Her righteousness is attested. Yes, she is barren, but her piety is vindicated. Posterity is not the ultimate expression of God's love, despite Hannah's intense desire to bear a son. However, her desire for a child remains, and she is not satisfied with her husband's consolation. Trevor Dennis describes her next course of action: "Unable to get any help or true sympathy from her husband, she turns to the one who *is* at the centre of all things, who will surely understand her, and who can, if he so chooses, enable her to have a child. She turns to God."[9]

Hannah weeps and prays in bitterness of soul: "O Lord of hosts, if thou wilt indeed look on the affliction of thine handmaid, and remember me, and not forget thine handmaid, but wilt give unto thine handmaid a man child, then I will give him unto the Lord all the days of his life, and there shall no razor come upon his head" (1 Samuel 1:11).[10]

The version of Hannah's prayer found in the Bible differs from the one in *Biblical Antiquities*. In 1 Samuel 1:11, Hannah makes a vow[11] that she will return her son to God's service if her petition is granted. Pseudo-Philo omits Hannah's vow and replaces it with her declaration of the sovereignty of God's will in all things, from the ruling of the heavens to the opening and closing of the wombs of the world, including her own. Hannah reminds God that she has served him all her life and begs him to grant her entreaty.

> And Hannah prayed and said, "Did you not, Lord, search out the heart of all generations before you formed the world? Now what womb is born opened or dies closed unless you wish it? And now let my prayer ascend before you today lest I go down from here empty, because you know my heart, how I have walked before you from the day of my youth. (50:4)

Pseudo-Philo also includes a revelation of Hannah's inner turmoil and her struggles to understand why God has not answered her heartfelt pleas. Hannah speculates that God's silent response to her passionate petition will reflect poorly on God's reputation for mercy upon his faithful followers.

> And Hannah did not want to pray out loud as all people do. For then she thought, saying, "Perhaps I am not worthy to be heard, and Peninnah will then be even more eager to taunt me as she does daily when she says, 'Where is your God in whom you trust?' And I know that neither she who has many sons is rich, nor she who has few is poor, but whoever abounds in the will of God is rich. For who may know what I have prayed for? If they know that I am not heard in my prayer, they will blaspheme." (50:5)

This passage once again emphasizes Peninnah's daily taunts, but this theme is superseded by Hannah's concern that God not be blasphemed. She feels that her barrenness reflects on God. Although Hannah has observed God's laws faithfully, people may feel that he has not kept his covenantal promises to her. Peninnah has already concluded that God has abandoned Hannah. Peninnah taunts her daily, not only because she is childless but also because God has not responded to her petition.[12]

Hateful as Peninnah might be, and as insensitive as the well-meaning Elkanah can sometimes be, Hannah's concern is with God's vindication. She trusts him. She does not want others to look at her and say, "Hannah is devoted to God. And yet, despite her piety, God has closed her womb. What kind of a God is that?" In spite of a trial that might threaten the faith of many pious women, Hannah's anguish actually serves the opposite purpose. It drives her to have remarkable, relentless faith. The Hannah who weeps and pleads with God is anything but hard and cold toward him. Although she easily *could* feel that God has abandoned her, it is clear from her prayer that she has not abandoned God. She realizes that Peninnah's taunting is as disrespectful to God as it is painful to her. Even more than she wants a son, she wants God to vindicate himself as the God who hears and answers the prayers of those who trust him. She willingly offers her most priceless treasure, her unborn son, to close the mouth of one who dared to mock her God. Hannah is an *ezer*. She is strong. She does all she can to maintain the faith that will enable God to rule over his enemies. She stands "squarely in the path of those who [mock] him and [fights] to take back the honor and praise that rightfully [belongs] to him. She "[offers] up Samuel before he [is] even conceived."[13]

Readers may wonder why Pseudo-Philo has chosen to leave out

Hannah's vow to dedicate her son to God, since it is such a central feature in the biblical account. One apparent explanation is that there is no need for it, since the child has already been promised to the people of Israel. The answer to Hannah's prayer and the answer to the nation's prayers are one and the same. The priest Eli declares to Hannah: "You have not asked alone, but the people have prayed for this. This is not your request alone, but it was promised previously to the tribes" (51:2). The elimination of the vow changes the miracle of Samuel's birth from a blessing for one righteous woman to the fulfillment of a foreordained promise that was made to an entire nation. Hannah, however, is unaware of the great significance of God's pledge to his people.

Pseudo-Philo emphasizes that Eli does "not want to tell her that a prophet [has] been foreordained to be born from her" (50:7). Only when Samuel is dedicated to the Lord does Eli tell Hannah of the significance of her son's birth (51:2).[14] Eli apparently withholds from Hannah the fact that she will bear a son. The text is probably presented this way in order to emphasize Hannah's faithfulness to God despite trying circumstances. Hannah is a model of devotion and is worthy of emulation for her patient faith in the surety of God's benevolence. Her example would be less compelling if, at this point, she knew her plea would be answered.

Hannah's prayer is the first time in the Bible that a barren woman has petitioned God for a child. As far as we know, the earlier matriarchs in the Old Testament did not turn to prayer as a way to overcome their barrenness. Sarah takes it upon herself to substitute Hagar's womb for her own. Rachel does not turn to God but to her husband and demands, "Give me children, or else I die" (Genesis 30:1). Jacob reminds her to whom she should have appealed by asking, "Am I in God's stead?" (Genesis 30:2). In Rebecca's case, there is a prayer offered, but it is Isaac who offers it on her behalf.

Hannah, however, does not depend on Elkanah to pray for her. Her prayer is the only prayer by a woman in the entire Old Testament that is quoted for us to read. Eve, Sarah, and Hagar converse with God, and Rebecca "enquires of the Lord" (Genesis 25:22) but their words are not recorded. There are numerous accounts in the stories of the Apocrypha where significant prayers are uttered by women, but not in the Old Testament. Hannah's vow is also unique. Her readiness to hand over her long-anticipated son places her on a par with Abraham being ready to sacrifice Isaac on Mount Moriah (Genesis 22).[15]

Hannah is also the first layperson to pray in any sanctuary. At this point in history, before institutionalized prayer replaced sacrifice as the means of public worship, Hannah becomes a model for "the prayer of the heart." Although all she wants to do is communicate the desires of her heart to God and be heard, the results of her appeal is both spiritual and political. Later rabbis were so impressed with Hannah's prayer and her defense of it to Eli, that they interjected the following words into the Bible story:

> Hannah said to [Eli]: You are no person of authority in this matter, and the Spirit of Holiness is not upon you, since you have been suspicious of me in this matter... You are no person of authority, nor is the Divine Presence of the Spirit of Holiness with you, since you have presumed me guilty rather than innocent. Are you not aware that I am a woman in anguish?" (*Babylonian Talmud, Tractate Berakhot* 31b).[16]

In order to fully understand Hannah's conversations with the priest Eli, we need to review the nature of Israelite religious observance. As the Psalms reveal, these celebrations were animated, sometimes raucous, affairs. Pilgrimages "provided for most people some of the few occasions during the year when they could eat meat in any quantity and drink wine freely."[17] The high priest of the sanctuary at Shiloh mistakes Hannah's passionate behavior for drunkenness. Without this background knowledge about Israelite festivals, we might have thought Eli's words offensive, but now they seem somewhat understandable. However, this is the second time that a man has observed Hannah's distress and not understood it. Elkanah thinks he knows what is going on and is well-meaning in his compassion but inept at providing comfort. Eli also believes he knows what is going on and fails to show kindness. We wonder at his concern over the apparently drunken woman when he turns a blind eye to the contemptible actions and corruption of his own two sons in 1 Samuel 2.

Hannah's conversations with the priest Eli at Shiloh in *Biblical Antiquities* correspond roughly with the account in 1 Samuel. Eli assumes that she is drunk because he sees Hannah's lips move but does not hear her words. He rebukes her for being in the temple in such a state. Pseudo-Philo expands this exchange to include references to Peninnah's taunting of Hannah. Eli asks her, "Tell me why you are being taunted" (50:7), even though Hannah has not mentioned the issue. She responds by reciting to him that "God had shut up [her] womb." She says, "I have prayed before him that I do not go forth from this world without fruit and that I do not die without having my own image." Eli assures her, "Go, because I know for what you have prayed; your prayer has been heard" (50:7). He does not elaborate on how he knows this or how her request will be fulfilled. Hannah returns home, "consoled of her sorrow," but without telling anyone "for what she [has] prayed" (50:8).

The story continues in *Biblical Antiquities* much as it does in 1 Samuel 1:20–28. Hannah conceives, bears a son, and names him Samuel.[18] She nurses him at home for two years until he is weaned, at which time she takes him to Shiloh to be dedicated to the service of the Lord:

> So the woman abode, and gave her son suck until she weaned him. And when she had weaned him, she took him up with her, with three bullocks, and one ephah of flour, and a bottle of wine, and brought him unto the house of the Lord in Shiloh: and the child was young. And they slew a bullock, and brought the child to Eli. And she said, . . . I am the woman that stood by thee here, praying unto the Lord. For this child I prayed; and the Lord hath given me my petition which I asked of him: Therefore also I have lent him to the Lord; as long as he liveth he shall be lent to the Lord. And he worshiped the Lord there. (1 Samuel 1:23–28)

In the biblical narrative, Hannah is the single subject of the account until verse 25 when the plural pronoun *they* appears and we can assume that Elkanah is also present. In his account, Pseudo-Philo omits the references to Elkanah and the sacrificial offerings. Hannah's portrayal in the account is noteworthy because she appears as an independent and dependable person who is competent in carrying out the decisions she has determined to be honorable. "And Hannah remained there and nursed the infant until he was two years old. And when she had weaned him, she went up with him and brought gifts in her hands. And the child was very handsome, and the Lord was with him" (51:1). Hannah is solely responsible for her son.

In *Biblical Antiquities,* Eli responds to Hannah's profession that her young son is the answer to her prayer by divulging the full magnitude of Samuel's birth. He emphasizes the people's role in this occurrence and its far-reaching ramifications. Eli replies: "You have not asked alone, but the people have prayed for this. This is not your request alone, but it was promised previously to the tribes. And through this boy your womb has been justified so that you might provide advantage for the peoples and set up the milk of your breasts as a fountain for the twelve tribes" (51:2). Eli addresses both the meaning of Samuel's birth for Hannah and for the nation at large. Hannah has prayed for a son. Israel has prayed for a ruler. These prayers have converged and Samuel is the answer to both petitions. Hannah has been vindicated by the birth of her child. She knows that God has not abandoned her. Similarly, Israel has also been vindicated. Samuel's birth is proof that God has not rejected them or left them to themselves.[19]

Everyone loves happy endings. We all rejoice with Hannah over Samuel's birth. We empathize with the agony Hannah must feel as she delivers her son to Shiloh. When she returns home, the silence there must be deafening. It is no longer ringing with the laughter of a toddler. She is no longer able to tuck him in and help him say his prayers and no longer be able to take his little hand in hers. She must have a gaping hole in her heart at this time. So what is the explanation for her joy? She does not know yet that she will bear five more children—three sons and two daughters. She has given away her most precious possession. How can she be joyful? Hannah understands something. She understands that she lives in a world where nothing is beyond the reach of God's reign. She realizes that even though she is a child of God, she will not be spared the painful side of life. She has experienced suffering, despite the enormity of her faith. She has been assaulted by doubt, depression, and fear. But, she realizes that God uses the hard experiences of life to make us strong. She says, "They that stumbled are girded with strength" (1 Samuel 2:4).

Hannah is stalwart *because* she had stumbled and fallen flat on her face. She turns to God instead of turning away. When she speaks to God, it is as though she is reminding herself that he already has her welfare in mind. By giving thanks to God, Hannah prods herself to remember that God is in control of the events in her life that have caused her such misery. She knows he loves her. Therefore, she asks herself what she needs to learn from her circumstances. How is he at work in her life to make her stronger? She probably would not have guessed that through all her tribulations, God is preparing her to raise one of Israel's greatest prophet-leaders—the counselor to Israel's first kings.[20]

Hannah responds to Eli's disclosure about the meaning of Samuel's birth in the form of a hymn. In the biblical account, it takes the form of a prayer:

> And Hannah prayed, and said, My heart rejoiceth in the Lord, mine horn is exalted in the Lord: my mouth is enlarged over mine enemies; because I rejoice in thy salvation. There is none holy as the Lord: for there is none beside thee: neither is there any rock like our God. Talk no more so exceeding proudly; let not arrogancy come out of your mouth: for the Lord is a God of knowledge, and by him actions are weighed. The bows of the mighty men are broken, and they that stumbled are girded with strength. They that were full have hired out themselves for bread; and they that were hungry ceased: so that the barren hath born seven; and she that hath many children is waxed feeble. The Lord killeth, and maketh alive: he bringeth down to the grave, and bringeth up. The Lord maketh poor, and maketh rich: he bringeth low, and lifteth up. He raiseth up the poor out of the dust, and lifteth up the beggar from the dunghill, to set them among princes, and to make them inherit the throne of glory: for the pillars of the earth are the Lord's, and he hath set the world upon them. He will keep the feet of his saints, and the wicked shall be silent in darkness; for by strength shall no man prevail. The adversaries of the Lord shall be broken to pieces; out of heaven shall he thunder upon them: the Lord shall judge the ends of the earth; and he shall give strength unto his king, and exalt the horn of his anointed. (1 Samuel 2:1–10)

Although there are some parallels to the biblical prayer, Hannah's hymn in *Biblical Antiquities* is more like the Hymn of Deborah in *Biblical Antiquities* 32. Pseudo-Philo creates this anthem in order to emphasize that Samuel is both an answer to Hannah's prayer for a son and to Israel's plea for a leader. Hannah supplicates,

Come to my voice, all you nations,
and pay attention to my speech, all you kingdoms,
because my mouth has been opened that I should speak
and my lips have been commanded to sing a hymn to the Lord.
Drip, my breasts, and tell your testimonies,
because you have been commanded to give milk.
For he who is milked from you will be raised up,
and the people will be enlightened by his words,
and he will show to the nations the statutes,
and his horn will be exalted very high.
And so I will speak my words openly,
because from me will arise the ordinance of the Lord,
and all men will find the truth. (51:3–4)

In this section, Pseudo-Philo once again makes a comparison between words and milk. Hannah's mouth has been commanded to speak words. She commands her breasts to drip milk and "tell your testimonies." Hannah speaks as a prophetess deserving the attention of the nation. She acknowledges the mighty works of Israel's God in the past and in the future. She emphasizes the role of her son in Israel's future and her own role in accomplishing God's purposes.

The next section of Hannah's hymn highlights the reversal of fortunes for both the righteous and the wicked and the destiny of each. This passage closely parallels its biblical corollary:

Do not hurry to say great things
or to bring forth from your mouth lofty words,
but delight in glorifying (God).
For when the light from which wisdom is to be born will go forth,
not those who possess many things will be said to be rich,
nor those who have borne in abundance will be called mothers.
For the sterile one has been satisfied in childbearing,
but she who had many children has been emptied.
Because the Lord kills in judgment,
and brings to life in mercy.
For them who are wicked in this world he kills,
and he brings the just to life when he wishes.
Now the wicked he will shut up in darkness,
but he will save his light for the just.
And when the wicked have died, then they will perish.

And when the just go to sleep then they will be freed.
Now so will every judgment endure,
until he who restrains will be revealed. (51:4–5)

In this section, Pseudo-Philo draws a sharp contrast between the allusions to wealth, posterity, and abundance on one hand and destitution, sterility, and barrenness on the other. All who wait upon God will be vindicated and receive their just rewards.

Hannah continues with her hymn in *Biblical Antiquities* 51:6:

Speak, speak, Hannah, and do not be silent.
Sing a hymn, daughter of Batuel,
about the miracles that God has performed with you.
Who is Hannah that a prophet is born from her?
Or who is the daughter of Batuel that she should bear the light to
the peoples?

Here, Hannah exhorts herself to openly expound the miracles that God has performed through her. She need be silent no longer because God has vindicated her through giving her a son. He has also shown his mercy to Israel through her, by giving them a long-anticipated guide and spiritual leader.

Hannah next addresses her husband, Elkanah:

Rise up, you also, Elkanah, and gird your loins.
Sing a hymn about the wonders of the Lord.
Because Asaph prophesied in the wilderness about your son,
saying,
'Moses and Aaron were among his priests,
and Samuel was there among them.'
Behold the word has been fulfilled,
and the prophecy has come to pass.
And these words will endure
until they give the horn to his anointed one
and power be present at the throne of his king. (51:6)

This section of the hymn has no parallel in 1 Samuel except for the last two lines. It emphasizes that Samuel will provide enlightened guidance to the people until the commencement of the reign of God's "anointed one." Hannah is strikingly portrayed as a leader in worship, exhorting even her husband to praise God. She expounds the meaning of scriptures to him and discerns the significance of Samuel's birth. In doing this she resembles Deborah, who ascertains God's will and takes over leadership from Barak even during the victory celebration after the battle. Once again, a capable, righteous woman takes over the spiritual leadership when we would expect a man to do so.[21]

Hannah's hymn will be treasured and cherished in Israel for many years. Mary, the mother of the Lord, will know it by heart as a young girl from the hill country of Judea. Luke will put phrases from it into Mary's psalm as she praises God for what he has done for her. Hannah's words deserve to be heard by the entire world as she articulates what she has learned about God. She once prayed in silence, but now her voice is bold and sure.[22]

Hannah must have had moments when she wondered if her faith would survive. That's how she discovers that God will "keep the feet of his saints" (1 Samuel 2:9). How else can we explain Hannah's actions in the face Peninnah's constant ridicule, her extended infertility, and God's apparent abandonment? Why else, when God's silence pushes her to the edge of a spiritual cliff, would Hannah turn to God instead of turning away? She is at the end of her rope and is hanging on with her faith. Hannah is clinging to God, but God is holding onto her even more firmly.[23]

Hannah's name comes from the Hebrew root *h-n-n* and has two possible meanings. The primary meaning of this root is "to be gracious" or "to show favor." Her name thus interpreted shows the eventual blessings and fertility she receives from the Lord. Another meaning of this root is "to be loathsome." Peninnah fulfills this meaning with her daily taunting and terrible treatment. Hannah's name encapsulates the story of her life—at first she is wretched, and then she receives favor from God. She herself shows graciousness in mothering her son, making great sacrifices for his sake.[24] Leila Leah Bronner writes of the connections between the meaning of Hannah's name and prayer:

> The rabbis also attribute to her the quality of grace, which fits with the primary meaning of her name, "to show favor" or to "be gracious." To extend upon this etymology, the secondary meaning of her name—"yearn toward," "long for," "be merciful," "be compassionate," "be favorable," "incline toward," "seek or implore favor"—all suggest the phenomenon of prayer. Some meanings,

such as "yearn toward," express the posture of the suppliant; others, the attitude hoped for on the part of the deity. The meaning "long for" also fits exactly Hannah's long years of longing for a child—the impetus for her prodigious act of prayer.[25]

What Hannah learns through her barrenness is a rock-solid theology that prepared her prophet-son for his mission in life. His young heart soaks up his mother's love for God and her conviction that God keeps "the feet of his saints" (1 Samuel 2:9). As I have already noted, Hannah lives in a time when Israel's leadership is uncertain. The people are apathetic about God. The priesthood is deplorably corrupt. Hannah comes forth as a spiritual leader when this caliber of righteous guidance is hopelessly deficient in Israel. The strength of character she develops during her years as a barren woman is passed on to Samuel as he endeavors to lead the people during an arduous time in their history—the corruption and fall of Eli's sons, the anointing and decline of King Saul, and the rise of King David to power. Hannah's teachings sustain Samuel through all of these perils, as well as the people's painful rejection of him in their plea for a king. Hannah's theology has made its way into the hearts of Israel's kings through her son's influence over them. Many Old Testament scholars believe Hannah was the theologian for the monarchy.[26]

When the time comes for Samuel to be dedicated, Hannah dresses him and takes him to the sanctuary. Even though he no longer lives under her roof, she watches him grow up from a distance. Every year Hannah sews a little robe for Samuel to wear under his priestly clothing and delivers it to him when she visits Shiloh on the annual family pilgrimage (1 Samuel 2:19). This loving act bespeaks Hannah's abiding love and influence in Samuel's life. Through her influence and dedication, Hannah has decisive influence over Samuel, one of Israel's foremost spiritual leaders. "This influence demonstrates the power if not the authority of biblical women."[27]

Notes

1. Trevor Dennis, *Sarah Laughed* (Nashville: Abingdon Press, 1994), 116.
2. Cheryl Anne Brown, *No Longer Be Silent: First Century Jewish Portraits of Biblical*

Women (Louisville: Westminster/John Knox Press, 1992), 145; see also Dennis, *Sarah Laughed*, 117.

3. Brown, *No Longer Be Silent: First Century Jewish Portraits of Biblical Women*, 147.

4. Dennis, *Sarah Laughed*, 119.

5. William Shakespeare, *Hamlet*, act 3, scene 2.

6. Dennis, *Sarah Laughed*, 123.

7. The Hebrew meaning of this passage is unclear. Scholars and translators have come up with various suggestions: that she is given the best part of the animal, that she is given a double portion, or that she has a single one which is equivalent to the total amount given to Peninnah and her children. See Dennis, *Sarah Laughed*, 119–20.

8. Carolyn Curtis James, *Lost Women of the Bible* (Grand Rapids: Zondervan, 2005), 125.

9. Dennis, *Sarah Laughed*, 122–23.

10. Hannah is promising to dedicate the son for whom she is praying as a nazarite. *Nazar* is a Hebrew word that means "to separate" and the terms for making a nazarite vow are laid out in Numbers 6:1–21. A nazarite was "set apart" or consecrated to the service of God and denoted that commitment to God by such things as not cutting his or her hair, or not drinking wine or partaking of the fruit of the vine. See Dennis, *Sarah Laughed*, 124.

11. When Hannah informs Elkanah of her plans to dedicate Samuel to the Lord in the biblical narrative, he says, "Do what seemeth thee good" (1 Samuel 1:23). Hannah has not asked Elkanah to confirm her vow. He apparently does not even know she has *made* a vow. She informs him of her plan to dedicate Samuel to the Lord as if it is a decision she has already made. Hannah takes the initiative, and all the actions taken will be hers alone—apart from actually performing the sacrifices for Samuel's dedication, in which, as a woman, she could not take part. See Dennis, *Sarah Laughed*, 130.

12. Brown, *No Longer Be Silent: First Century Jewish Portraits of Biblical Women*, 151.

13. James, *Lost Women of the Bible*, 127–31.

14. Brown, *No Longer Be Silent: First Century Jewish Portraits of Biblical Women*, 152.

15. Dennis, *Sarah Laughed*, 124–25.

16. Megan McKenna, *Leave Her Alone* (Maryknoll, New York: Orbis Books, 2000), 37.

17. Dennis, *Sarah Laughed*, 119.

18. Hannah names the boy herself. Only she and God know the terms of her vow. Only she sees the child as the answer to her prayer, and that is the meaning of his name—"an answer to prayer." The name Samuel is connected in this story with the Hebrew word *sa'al*, meaning "to ask." See Dennis, *Sarah Laughed*, 129.

19. Brown, *No Longer Be Silent: First Century Jewish Portraits of Biblical Women*, 155.

20. James, *Lost Women of the Bible*, 134.

21. Brown, *No Longer Be Silent: First Century Jewish Portraits of Biblical Women*, 161.

22. McKenna, *Leave Her Alone*, 35.

23. James, *Lost Women of the Bible*, 134.

24. Leila Leah Bronner, *Stories of Biblical Mothers: Maternal Power in the Hebrew Bible* (Lanham: University Press of America, 2004), 33.

25. Leila Leah Bronner, *From Eve to Esther: Rabbinic Reconstructions of Biblical Women* (Louisville, Kentucky: Westminster John Knox Press, 1994), 97.

26. James, *Lost Women of the Bible*, 137.

27. Bronner, *Stories of Biblical Mothers: Maternal Power in the Hebrew Bible*, 32–33.

CHAPTER 10
Hagar: Not Forgotten by God
Genesis 12–16

WE IN THE WEST, WHO come from the European tradition, remember little in the Bible about a woman named Hagar. Islamic tradition says that she is the mother of their tribe and that Ishmael, not Isaac, was the one Abraham was going to sacrifice. By the time Hagar appears on the scene in the Abraham story, she is already at the bottom of the social ladder. Genesis 16:1 tells us that Abraham's wife, Sarai, has "an handmaid, an Egyptian, whose name [is] Hagar." Hagar is a slave and a foreigner. We don't think too much about the statement. Lots of people had slaves in the ancient world. We infer that she was probably given to Sarai while she and her husband were in Egypt during the famine. She was probably a gift from the Pharaoh.[1] "And [Pharaoh] entreated Abram well for [Sarai's] sake: and he had sheep, and oxen, and he asses, and menservants, and *maidservants*, and she asses, and camels" (Genesis 12:16, emphasis added).

Hagar is part of Abraham's property—cut off from her family and her country, completely alone in the world, and without anyone to look out for her personal interests. She has no rights or power of her own.

She must do the bidding of her mistress. If Sarai treats Hagar kindly, then her life might be tolerable. If Sarai does not, Hagar has no means of redress. She is always subject to the whims of others.

The Lord tells Abram that "he that shall come forth out of thine own bowels shall be thine heir" (Genesis 15:4). Sarai, who is still childless after decades of marriage, is desperate for a child. She can see no other means to provide Abram with an heir, except to give him her slave Hagar as a second wife. The advantage for the wife in such an arrangement is that the wife retains control of the slave and, if she desires, of the slave's child as long as her husband lives.[2]

Hagar does not even have rights over her own body. She is simply informed of her mistress's plan to be used as a surrogate mother so that Sarai might "obtain children by her." Sarai tells Abram, "Behold now, the Lord hath restrained me from bearing: I pray thee, go in unto my maid; it may be that I may obtain children by her. And Abram hearkened to the voice of Sarai. And Sarai Abram's wife took Hagar her maid the Egyptian . . . and gave her to her husband Abram to be his wife" (Genesis 16:2–3).

The King James Version of the Bible does not translate the Hebrew for "might obtain children by her" literally in verse 2. The Hebrew literally says, "that I might be 'built up' through her."[3] Sarai intends to build her posterity through the medium of another woman's womb. If a wife is barren, she can obtain a child by having her husband conceive a child with her slave. At this moment, all we see is Hagar's powerlessness.[4] She is there to serve Abram and Sarai, and, at present, Sarai wants her to conceive a child.

When Hagar conceives, although her legal status has not changed, her social standing is radically altered. She has conceived, while Sarai is barren. In other places in the Old Testament, the announcement of conception is followed immediately afterward by the news of the birth. Not this time.

Unwisely, when Hagar "saw that she had conceived," she "despised" her mistress (Genesis 16:4). The Hebrew word *qalal* means "to be slight," or "trifling."[5] Not only is Hagar validated as a woman by her pregnancy, she is carrying Abram's child. Although her scornful reaction proves to be heartlessly insensitive to her mistress's feelings and extremely unwise, it reflects Hagar's first toehold of power over her own life—the first time she has triumphed in anything. Hagar and Sarai have been placed in a situation where conflict could be expected, yet it still brings tragic suffering upon both of them. When I was learning Chinese characters, I found it intriguing that the character that had a roof with one woman under it meant peace, but the character that had a roof with two women characters under it stood for chaos.

Apparently, this tension between wives was such a common problem that the Code of Hammurabi had a provision for it: "When a slave-wife upon conceiving or bearing children tried to elevate herself to the status of her mistress, her mistress could brand her with a slave mark and return her to the rank of a slave."[6]

Sarai feels a sense of her own failure and despair. She uses the word "violence" to describe her treatment by Hagar. Sarai suggests to Abram that he might share some of the blame. "And Sarai said unto Abram, My wrong [or violence] be upon thee: I have given my maid into thy bosom; and when she saw that she had conceived, I was despised in her eyes: the Lord judge between me and thee" (Genesis 16:5). *Chamac,* translated here as "wrong" or "violence," is the same word that is used to describe the rude wickedness of men before the flood.[7] Sarai consults Abram in this domestic turmoil, but he does nothing to resolve it. It seems that men have traditionally been reluctant to get involved in the emotions of women. Although Hagar bears his child and seemingly should warrant his protection, he does nothing. Abram simply reminds her of the law. He tells Sarai, his wife of many years, that it is *her* maidservant and she should do "as it pleaseth" her (Genesis 16:6). Although Hagar has a name, neither her mistress nor her mistress's husband has used it in this interchange—even though she carries the child of her mistress's husband.

Hagar's indiscreet moment of exultant victory results in such harsh treatment by Sarai that Hagar fears for her life and flees. Genesis 16:6 tells us that Sarai "dealt hardly with her." We do not know what Sarai did, but the Code of Hammurabi allowed an owner to scour the mouth of an insolent slave with a quart of salt.[8] Hagar's flight is the first thing she has done of her own volition. Everything else has been done *to* her.

We next see Hagar at a place near the Egyptian border where there is water. It is presumed she has decided to go home. She is "found" by the messenger of the Lord (16:7)—the kind of finding that results from earnestly looking for someone or something. We learn that this desert meeting is no chance encounter. "The messenger of the Lord" meets her, but we do not discover who he really is until the end of the episode. We are given clues. Trevor Dennis likens Hagar's experience here to future events at Mount Sinai. He calls it a "place where God is encountered and new promises are made and new demands given."[9] The messenger of the Lord reminds her that she is Sarai's slave and wonders what she is doing out in the desert on her own. He asks, "Hagar, Sarai's maid, whence camest thou? and whither wilt thou go?" (Genesis 16:8). It is the first time someone besides the narrator of the story has used her name. We can only imagine what the impact of such a personal recognition must have had on her. She answers, "I flee from the face of my mistress Sarai" (Genesis 16:8). Hagar answers truthfully, but she does not tell him the whole story.

At this point, we wonder what God will do next. Has he seen her suffering? Is he going to free her from her miserable state of servitude? Is he going to make all her sufferings and anguish of spirit right again? We hope so. Why else would he have come? His answer surprises us. He sends her back to her abusive mistress. "Return to thy mistress, and submit thyself under her hands," the messenger commands (Genesis 16:9). The King James translation of this verse is far too tame for the literal Hebrew which again uses *anah*, the potent verb of the "dealt harshly" in verse 6.[10] This must have seemed like a harsh and frightening command, but God's ways are not the ways of men or women, and he often asks his children to perform actions that are the opposite of their natural inclinations.

God has an amazing revelation for Hagar: "I will multiply thy seed exceedingly, that it shall not be numbered for multitude" (Genesis 16:10). These are the familiar words of the promises made to Abram in Genesis 12, 13, and 15. In Genesis 15:5 he tells Abram to "Look now toward heaven, and tell [count] the stars, if thou be able to number them: and he said unto him, So shall thy seed be." But so far, Abram has been the only person to hear such promises. God will repeat these same promises to Abraham's son Isaac and grandson Jacob, but to no one else. Hagar joins the great patriarchs of the house of Israel in hearing these promises, though she is a woman, a slave, and an Egyptian.[11]

"And the angel of the Lord said unto her, Behold, thou art with child, and shalt bear a son, and shalt call his name Ishmael; because the Lord hath heard thy affliction" (Genesis 16:11). There are several annunciation scenes in the Bible. God's revelation about the destiny of Hagar's son is the first, however, and it is made to a woman.

This announcement is echoed by God's words to Abram, now known as Abraham, in the next chapter:

> And God said, Sarah thy wife shall bear thee a son indeed; and thou shalt call his name Isaac: and I will establish my covenant with him for an everlasting covenant, and with his seed after him. And as for Ishmael, I have heard thee: Behold, I have blessed him, and will make him fruitful, and will multiply him exceedingly; twelve princes shall he beget, and I will make him a great nation. But my covenant will I establish with Isaac, which Sarah shall bear unto thee at this set time in the next year. (Genesis 17:19–21)

In Judges 13:3–5, "the angel of the Lord" also announces the birth of a son to Manoah's wife, who turns out to be the mother of Samson. The most famous parallel occurs when the prophet Isaiah announces to King Ahaz that "the Lord himself will give him a sign," and that "a virgin shall conceive, and bear a son, and shall call his name Immanuel" (Isaiah 7:14). There are a few others in the Old Testament, but the most familiar to us are the ones in the New Testament—when an angel tells Zachariah of the birth of his son John the Baptist, when the angel Gabriel tells Mary that she will bear Jesus, and when the angel appears to Joseph in Matthew and tells him that Mary's son is also God's son.

Since there are so few annunciation scenes in scripture, and since each is so significant, we can see what a great honor God pays to Hagar in Genesis 16. He has been especially mindful of her afflictions, and he tells her so. Hagar is a different woman from the one who has fled into the wilderness. She now knows that a power higher than herself notices her and that knowledge transforms her. She is now free in a way that returning to slavery can never eradicate. She is important to God, and this gives her a new sense of self-worth. If God wants her to go back, then she will go back. He must have a purpose in sending her back to Sarai, and Hagar will obey.

Hagar has learned that God has a plan for her. She has learned that she will bear a son. But Hagar brings back to Abram and Sarai much more than the news of the sex of her unborn child. She will tell them that God has named the child Ishmael, which means, "God hears." She will tell her story to Abram and Sarai and teach them things about God that they need to know: That God does indeed hear the cries of the suffering, the downcast, and the abandoned; that every human soul has dignity and worth. Hagar's new knowledge is empowering. If God is with her, she can survive anything.

At this point, Hagar has an unshakeable faith that she is important to God. But she still has much to learn about God's ways. Even so, the next thing she does is unprecedented in all the history of scripture. *She* gives God a name. She calls him *El Roi*, or "the God who sees me." This name expresses her bedrock conviction—that God's eye is upon her. Other people who have seen God have named the *place* where the vision took place, but have never dared to give God a name. When Jacob wrestles all night with God at the River Jabbok, he names the place *Peniel* or "the face of God" (Genesis 32:30). After coming close to sacrificing Isaac, but being given a ram to sacrifice instead, Abraham names the place *Jehovah-jireh*, or "The Lord Sees" (Genesis 22:14). Abraham's name is very similar to the name Hagar gives God, but he names the *place* where the incident occurred. Neither Abraham nor Jacob presumes to name *God*. Only Hagar does that. And, she does not wait until he has left the scene. She calls him by her name right to his face—"Thou God seest me" or "You are the God who sees me" (Genesis 16:13). I think Oprah Winfrey would say that Hagar had *chutzpah*.

Hagar must have had an intense spiritual experience because when it is over, she is surprised to find herself unscathed. She says, "Have I also here looked after him that seeth me?" or "Have I really seen God and remained alive after seeing him?" (16:13). Hagar's amazement at surviving her encounter is echoed by Jacob after his experience at Peniel: "I have seen God face to face, and my life is preserved" (Genesis 32:30). In Judges 13, Manoah says to his wife, "We shall surely die, because we have seen God" (13:22).

The bedrock knowledge that she matters to God empowers Hagar to return to Sarai. This action is probably the first free act of her life, aside from running away. Now she can share with her mistress the precious truth that God is mindful of every creature—including childless Sarai. He has the tender love of a parent for every one of his children, notwithstanding their circumstances. He cares about what happens to each one of them. Abram and Sarai know of God as the Almighty, the Master of the universe, and the Creator of heaven and earth, but Hagar now teaches them that he is a personal God as well. He is not only infinite but also intimate. He is omniscient, but he knows his children one by one.

Hagar's story, as related to Abram and Sarai regarding the nature of God, is interwoven with the oral tradition that is passed down from generation to generation until Moses finally writes it down. She still needs to learn more about God's promises and covenants, and who better to teach her than Abram, the "Friend of God"? (James 2:23). Even in light of her later expulsion, God is clearly sending her back to live with the two people who are best qualified to teach her about her newfound God. She will learn the truths Abraham will teach to Ishmael. She will be an eyewitness to the miracle of Sarah's late-life pregnancy and the birth of Isaac in fulfillment of God's commitment. All these things will expand her soul.

Unfortunately, Hagar's story does not end with peace and domestic tranquility. The conflict between Sarah and Hagar breaks out again at the feast celebrating the weaning of Isaac. Although Hagar kindled the first conflict herself, this time it is her son who sets off the fireworks. Although Hagar is not involved in the problem, she suffers the consequences. At the feast, Ishmael does something that makes Sarah feel concerned for Isaac's safety. "And Sarah saw the son of Hagar the Egyptian, which she had born unto Abraham, mocking. Wherefore she said unto Abraham, Cast out this bondwoman and her son: for the son of this bondwoman shall not be heir with my son, even with Isaac" (Genesis 21:9–10).

Genesis tells us that the matter is very distressing to Abraham. "And the thing was very grievous in Abraham's sight because of his son" (Genesis 21:11). The text here does not specify which son, but we assume it is Ishmael. The book of *Jubilees* in the *Old Testament*

Pseudepigrapha states that Abraham was saddened "because of his maidservant and because of his son that he should drive them away from him" (17:5). In addition, the listing of Abraham's ten trials in *Jubilees* 17:7 mentions Ishmael's expulsion and then makes a separate reference to Hagar's expulsion.

In the Genesis narrative, God attributes feelings to Abraham that he has not expressed, but that God perceives in his heart: "And God said unto Abraham, Let it not be grievous in thy sight because of the lad, and because of thy bondwoman; in all that Sarah hath said unto thee, hearken unto her voice; for in Isaac shall thy seed be called. And also of the son of the bondwoman will I make a nation, because he is thy seed" (Genesis 21:12–13). Unlike during Hagar's earlier encounter with God, God does not use Hagar's name here. Why this inconsistency? Trevor Dennis believes it is because of God's promises and the limits they keep:

> When he is in the presence of Sarah and Abraham, God inhabits the world of the promises to them and to their descendants, and is bound by them. Though he has fine things in store for Ishmael also, the richest of his blessings are reserved for Isaac and the people that will eventually spring from him. The land of Canaan will be for them, not for the Ishmaelites. The covenant and the relationship it expresses will be for them, not with the bedouin. Only the people of Israel will be given his Torah at Sinai. Only they will be given a David, and the promise that his dynasty will last for ever.[12]

Hagar has no part in these promises.[13] She has received promises of her own. But once she and Ishmael are fending for themselves, God does not fail to come to their rescue.

Heeding God's directive to do as Sarah desires, Abraham acts.[14] "And Abraham rose up early in the morning, and took bread, and a bottle of water, and gave it unto Hagar, putting it on her shoulder, and the child, and sent her away: and she departed, and wandered in the wilderness of Beer-sheba" (Genesis 21:14). Thanks to Abraham, she takes with her water and bread, the necessities of life, as they begin their wanderings in the desert. The water runs out, and Hagar knows it means death for her son. "And the water was spent in the bottle, and she cast the child under one of the shrubs. And she went, and sat her down over against him a good way off, as it were a bowshot: for she said, Let me not see the death of the child. And she sat over against him, and lift up her voice, and wept" (Genesis 21:15–16). Hagar's casting of her son under a bush is a sign of her love. All she can do now is provide some shade for him while she waits for him to die. She retreats a short distance so she will not have to hear too much of his suffering. She does not seem to care that she too will die. She is a mother, and her concern is for her child. Her desperate cry to be spared from witnessing the death of her child is the last we will hear from Hagar.

However bleak the circumstance appears, God does spare Hagar from what she fears most: "And God heard the voice of the lad; and the angel of God called to Hagar out of heaven, and said unto her, What aileth thee, Hagar? fear not; for God hath heard the voice of the lad where he is. Arise, lift up the lad, and hold him in thine hand; for I will make him a great nation" (Genesis 21:17–18).

By responding to the boy's cries, God also shows his concern for what Hagar is most anxious about herself. She is not focused on her own plight but only on her child's. By rescuing the child, God is rescuing the mother. She would want it that way. If he paid too much attention to her, she would point him in the direction of the child and tell him not to be worried about her.

When God has finished talking with her, he directs her to a nearby well and opens her eyes. She fills the skin with water and gives her son a drink. Once again she can think about Ishmael's future and the promises God has made to him. After this event, the scriptures tell us that Ishmael thrives in the desert and becomes an expert with the bow. Hagar is both a mother *and* a father to him. It is she who takes the initiative to find a wife for him from Egypt—from her own people. She is free to live her life as she wishes. When she was living with Sarah and Abraham, the only initiative she could take was to run away. She has nothing more to do with slavery. She has become free.

So, how does Hagar measure up as an *ezer*? Does she live up to Eve's legacy? Absolutely. She is the poster child for validating the outcasts, the downtrodden, the disappointed, the lonely, and the desperate. If she, Hagar, a slave, a foreigner, and a woman who is utterly alone in life can receive one-on-one attention from God, so can everyone. She is an *ezer* because she rescues the disenfranchised from feeling forgotten. She teaches all women that no matter their circumstances, they matter to God. She demonstrates to all women that no matter how lowly their status might be, God's eyes are upon them. When Hagar flees into the wilderness, desperate and alone, God reaches out to her and encompasses her in the arms of his love. He endows Hagar with the knowledge of her significance in the scheme of things, and this knowledge brings strength to her and to all women who identify with her. Every woman can know that the eyes of the "God Who Sees Me" are upon her unceasingly and that if she will learn to recognize his hand in her life, she can be assured that God is continually blessing her.

Notes

1. In the Targum of Genesis 16, we are told that, according to the Midrash, Hagar had been given to Abraham by her father, the Pharaoh of Egypt, who said, "My daughter had better be a slave in the house of Abram, than the mistress in any other." J. W. Etheridge, *The Targums of Onkelos and Jonathan ben Uzziel on the Pentateuch*, Genesis and Exodus (London: Longman, Green, Longman, and Roberts, 1862), 204.

2. James Baker, *Women's Rights in Old Testament Times* (Salt Lake City: Signature Books, 1992), 99–100, footnote 11.

3. The practice of surrogate mothering was an established practice for the people of ancient Israel and other nations of the Ancient Near East. Genesis has other examples—the barren Rachel gives her maid Bilhah to her husband Jacob, as does her older sister, Leah, give her maid Zilpah. The offspring of such unions were regarded not only as the children of the husbands who fathered them but also as the children of the original wives whose slaves the birth mothers were. Trevor Dennis, *Sarah Laughed* (Nashville: Abingdon Press, 1994), 43.

4. In the ancient world, the prevalence of polygyny meant that multiple wives and concubines were a commonplace occurrence and were often a necessity to preserve a family line, especially where the first wife was barren. Our modern notions of individual choice were completely alien to the ancient mind. Fathers arranged marriages, and seldom were young men and women consulted in the decision-making process. Carolyn Curtis James, *Lost Women of the Bible* (Grand Rapids: Zondervan, 2005), 86–89.

5. Frances Brown, *The New Brown–Driver–Briggs–Gesenius Hebrew and English Lexicon* (Peabody: Hendrickson Publishers, 1979), 886.

6. See Baker, *Women's Rights in Old Testament Times*, 81.

7. Ibid., 329. "And God looked upon the earth, and, behold, it was corrupt; for all flesh had corrupted his way upon the earth. And God said unto Noah, The end of all flesh is come before me; for the earth is filled with violence through them; and, behold, I will destroy them with the earth" (Genesis 6:12–13).

8. Baker, *Women's Rights in Old Testament Times*, 82.

9. Dennis, *Sarah Laughed*, 65.

10. Brown, *The New Brown–Driver–Briggs–Gesenius Hebrew and English Lexicon*, 776.

11. Dennis, *Sarah Laughed*, 67.

12. Dennis, *Sarah Laughed*, 75.

13. Perhaps Deuteronomy 32:8 can clarify why Hagar and her descendants are not part of the promises to the house of Israel: "When the most High divided to the nations their inheritance, when he separated the sons of Adam, he set the bounds of the people according to the number of the children of Israel." Acts 17:26–27 also sheds light on this idea: "And hath made of one blood all nations of men for to dwell on all the face of the earth, and hath determined the times before appointed, and the bounds of their habitation."

We may also need to consider the idea that perhaps Hagar received a different foreordained stewardship in the premortal life in accordance with the nature and character of her spirit. This idea is supported by the following scriptures:

Jeremiah 1:5–6: "Then the word of the Lord came unto me, saying, Before I formed thee in the belly I knew thee; and before thou camest forth out of the womb I sanctified thee, and I ordained thee a prophet unto the nations."

Deuteronomy 14:2: "For thou art an holy people unto the Lord thy God, and the Lord hath chosen thee to be a peculiar people unto himself, above all the nations that are upon the earth."

Genesis 17:5: Abraham is promised he will be the father of *many* nations, and Hagar's offspring will allow that prophecy to be fulfilled.

14. David Rothstein writes, "It is of interest that Qimhi, a Jewish commentator while, of course, following the biblical version, introduces the motif of household harmony (shalom ba'it in Hebrew) . . . in explaining Abraham's willingness to tolerate Sarai's treatment of Hagar." We today would say, "If mama ain't happy, ain't nobody happy." David Rothstein, "Text and Context: Domestic Harmony and the Depiction of Hagar in Jubilees," *Journal for the Study of the Pseudepigrapha*, 17.4 (2008), 250, footnote 23.

CHAPTER 11
Tamar: Maligned and Misunderstood
Genesis 38

PEOPLE TEND TO SKIP OVER Tamar's story in Sunday School classes. Similar to Lot's daughters, Tamar resorts to drastic measures to conceive a child. You might ask, "What good can be said about a brazen woman who takes things into her own hands and poses as a harlot in order to seduce her father-in-law?" But Tamar has been given a bad rap. If we correctly understand the story, we will understand why, later on, when Boaz (a direct descendant of Judah) takes Ruth to be his wife, the elders of Bethlehem give a blessing to the new couple that ends, "Let thy house be like the house of Pharez, whom Tamar bare unto Judah" (Ruth 4:12).

The story begins when Judah, the instigator of the plot among Jacob's sons to rid themselves of their brother Joseph, leaves his brethren in Hebron and travels west to Adullam. Perhaps he knows that his father never fully believed the fabricated story about Joseph's death and is unable to live near his family because of the remorse and guilt that he suffers. In Adullam, he marries a Canaanite woman, the daughter of Shua, and begins to live the Canaanite lifestyle, adopting their customs and practices. Three sons are born to this union—Er, Onan, and Shelah.

Judah chooses a wife for his firstborn son Er[1], a woman named Tamar who is presumably of Canaanite descent.[2] (However, the Targum on Genesis 38 states that Tamar is the daughter of a priest.[3]) Er doesn't turn out to be Tamar's prince charming, however. The Bible does not tell us exactly what Er does, but apparently he is "wicked in the sight of the Lord" and it so angers the Lord that the Lord takes his life, leaving Tamar a childless widow (Genesis 38:7–8).

Er's death shatters Tamar's expectation for a future living happily-ever-after in a house with a white picket fence, or at least with a well-constructed goat pen. She loses the status and protection that her marriage would have afforded her. In her ancient society, when a woman marries a firstborn son, she expects that her own firstborn son will one day take his father's place in the family power structure as the primary heir of his father's estate. As the wife and mother of future community leaders, she will become the matriarch of the extended family, enjoying social and economic prestige. Her husband will inherit a double portion of his father's estate—twice as much as any other heir. This enables him to take care of his added responsibilities as the birthright son, which included supporting any unmarried sisters or his widowed mother.

The ancient world had an emergency plan to save a childless, dead husband from extinction. Moses formalizes it later as the Levirate Law in Deuteronomy 25:5–10. (*Levir* is Latin for "husband's brother.") It appears to have already been an established custom in Judah's time. According to this custom, if a man died without a child, his brother would marry his widow and cause her to become pregnant. The son born from this levirate marriage bore the dead husband's name, inherited all his property, and continued as a link in an unbroken genealogical chain as if he were the biological son of the deceased husband.

It is in Judah's best interests to retain Tamar in the family and support this practice. If Tamar marries Er's brother and bears children, she will help to build the family's numerical strength and economic soundness, despite the death of her husband. From a legal standpoint, Tamar's marital obligation continues as long as her father-in-law lives.

She is not declared a widow and allowed to go "whither she pleases"[4] until both her husband and father-in-law are dead. If no other sons are available, the father-in-law might also fulfill the custom by marrying his son's widow. It does not matter if the brothers or father-in-law are already married. We may assume that an older brother was primarily responsible to marry his brother's widow and that the responsibility passed from there to a younger brother, who in turn passed it to his father. In this case, Onan is the first in line, then Shelah, and then, if all else failed, Judah.[5]

The responsibility for arranging a levirate marriage for Tamar belongs to Judah. If he does not provide a son or himself as a husband, then she has the prerogative to demand that one of them do his duty. This is a right based on custom rather than codified civil laws. Therefore, a brother-in-law can choose to accept or reject the request of his sister-in-law without worrying about legal punishments. If he refuses her, his only consequence is public humiliation for failing to perform his familial duty.

Judah makes arrangements for Onan to marry Tamar. While the purpose of the levirate marriage is to raise up seed for the deceased brother and thus preserve his name, Onan is not so sure this course of action will be beneficial for him financially. The death of Er has greatly increased Onan's share of the family estate. Additionally, he is now entitled to the double portion of the firstborn son. Before Er's death he was entitled to 25 percent of his father's wealth. That number has just jumped to 66.6 percent. If Tamar bears a son, Onan will lose this extra inheritance. The law compels him to father the child that will sustain his brother's name and block his own sons from inheritance. To resolve this conflict of interests, Assyrian law specifies that the father-in-law, and not one of the brothers, is to act as the "wedding coordinator" for his daughter-in-law.

When the three parties—Judah, Tamar, and Onan—reach an agreement, the marriage becomes valid as soon as it is consummated. This sort of union required no dowry and no new marriage contract because all the arrangements of the first marriage remained in force.

Presumably, Onan's reasoning in the matter goes like this: knowing he can not openly defy a directive of his father, an act which could leave him disinherited, he connives to delude his father and cheat

Tamar. He only *pretends* to do the honorable thing by marrying Tamar and having sexual relations with her, but each time they are together, he spills his semen on the ground to prevent Tamar from conceiving a child. We can only imagine how appalling and humiliating this must be for Tamar, but what can she do? Go and tell Judah what his son is doing? She is powerless to do anything about Onan's deception. But God has a reputation for coming to the aid of the powerless, and once God steps in, Onan is outmaneuvered. Genesis 38:9–10 reports: "And Onan knew that the seed should not be his; and it came to pass, when he went in unto his brother's wife, that he spilled it on the ground, lest that he should give seed to his brother. And the thing which he did displeased the Lord: wherefore he slew him also." Suddenly Judah is down to one living son.

Since Judah's only remaining son is not "grown," indicating that he has not reached puberty, Judah orders Tamar to go to her father's house and live as a widow "till Shelah my son be grown" (Genesis 38:11). This arrangement signifies an oral contract that Shelah will become her levirate husband when he comes of age. In any case, Tamar is pushed out of her home and sent back to live with her parents. Such an action is irregular in this period of time and compromises Tamar's position. As a childless widow in her father's house, she is an unwanted burden with no social standing. She has no financial security, being cut off from her husband's family and inheritance.

It is clear that Judah does not release Tamar from her levirate duty at this time. He readily admits he is afraid that the woman one author has nicknamed "Toxic Tamar"[6] will cause him to lose his third son as well: "For he said, Lest peradventure [Shelah] die also, as his brethren did" (38:11). Despite his fears, he certainly does not want to risk losing his daughter-in-law as well as her dowry.[7] So, Judah does not arrange the new marriage, and he does not release her as an independent widow. She is forbidden to marry someone else as long as the brother of her dead husband is alive. Tamar is in limbo. She has become an economic albatross around her father's neck. She is a pariah in her father's house as well as in Judah's house. Wearing the black attire of a widow, she lives in chaste spinsterhood and watches her childbearing years tick away.

Carolyn Curtis James notes that historians have discovered ancient Hittite and Assyrian laws that governed the levirate obligation. "These documents," she writes, "not only placed responsibility on the brother of the deceased but . . . also supported marriage of the father-in-law to his son's widow if no brother fulfilled this duty." Later, the law of Moses prohibited such marriages between father-in-law and daughter-in-law, but in Judah's time, the father-in-law bore responsibility for keeping his son's name alive. According to such statutes, conceiving a child by a father-in-law constituted a legitimate way to preserve a son's name from extinction.[8]

Tamar waits. Years pass, and Judah's wife dies. Shelah grows to manhood, yet there is no sign from Tamar's father-in-law that he is going to give Shelah to her as a husband as promised. At this time, women are not encouraged to be straightforward, so she cannot confront Judah directly about not keeping his word. Once convinced of Judah's intention to keep Shelah[9] from her, Tamar seems to change into a different person. Before this time, she has passively waited for things to happen. She has let herself be acted upon, but now she determines to take action herself. When she hears that Judah is on his way to shear his sheep at Timnath, she determines to seize the window of opportunity and make her move.[10] She tosses aside her widow's clothes and disguises herself as a cult prostitute.

Cult prostitutes were common in the ancient Near East. They were women who offered their "services" to would-be-takers and donated their earnings to the temple. Genesis uses two different Hebrew words to refer to Tamar on the road to Timnah. The word for harlot as we understand it today is *zonah*. This word is used first, and later the word *kedeshah* is used, which means "consecrated woman" and refers to a female associated with cult worship. Tamar probably knows that Judah is likely to visit a cult prostitute at shearing time.[11] Apparently, he has adopted this custom in order to ensure the increase of his herds during his sojourn in Adullam. Tamar knows Judah well enough to know that the plan she has concocted will be successful. She presses Judah to do what he *should* have done by engineering events that will lead to his fulfilling the law.

Tamar knows that many men visit prostitutes during the celebrations that accompany the sheep-shearing season. She proceeds to Enaim and selects a spot at the crossroads where Judah will certainly see her as he travels to Timnah. In Hebrew, the word "crossroads" is *em haderech*, or "the mother of roads," and is an ageless metaphor for encountering a crucial decision. Indeed, both Tamar and Judah make a crucial decision at this crossroads.

I wonder if Tamar considers all the things that could go wrong with her plan. Does she consider the possible risks to her life as well as to her honor? What if someone besides Judah propositions her? What if it is not the right time of her cycle to permit conception? What if someone speaks out against her as a prostitute? Apparently, she decides that her stratagem is worth the risk.

Judah sees Tamar dressed in a veil (which apparently signals her position as a *kedesah*) and asks permission to lie with her. "I pray thee, let me come in unto thee" (Genesis 38:16). Tamar skillfully negotiates the price, letting him set the terms. "What wilt thou give me, that thou mayest come in unto me? And he said, I will send thee a kid from the flock" (38:16–17). Judah must be acting spontaneously, because he does not have the promised kid with him. Tamar asks for a pledge that he will keep his word, this time cleverly setting the terms herself. She stipulates that he leave his seal, cord, and staff. The seal, or signet, was an engraved ring or cylinder made of metal or stone that had distinctive markings on it. A man often wore it around his neck on a cord. He used the seal to emboss his personal stamp on official documents. The staff would have been carved with unique markings showing that it belonged to Judah. He entrusts these valuable items willingly to Tamar, showing the high regard given such "consecrated women." To leave his signet and cord with her is the modern equivalent of giving her his driver's license. Judah lies with her, and afterward she leaves the scene and returns to her father's house to change back into her widow's garb. Once again, she waits.

Judah later sends his friend Hirah the Adullamite to deliver the kid and recover his personal items, but the woman is nowhere to be found. No one seems to know anything about a *kedeshah* in that area, and Hirah returns empty-handed to Judah. Judah stews because he doesn't want to be known as a man who doesn't pay his debts—never mind that he visits prostitutes. We raise our eyebrows at this seeming inconsistency, but he is obeying the priorities of his time and place. He has a witness that he *tried* to render payment, Hirah the Adullamite. He goes on with his life. He just wants to make sure he is not a laughingstock in the community. After all, he has his pride. He can't stress over one woman he met on the side of the road. The matter is done with.[12]

Three months later, Judah learns through the grapevine that Tamar is pregnant. Keep in mind that she is the childless widow of both Er and Onan and has been promised in levirate marriage to Shelah. Such an obligation carries a similar legal status to a betrothal. Tamar's pregnancy is proof of her adultery, since Shelah has not touched her. Tamar's condition will bring shame to Judah's whole family. She must be punished publicly in order to restore the family's honor. Judah calls for her to be brought forth and burned.[13] The usual punishment for an adulterous woman is to be stoned to death. Being burned to death is reserved for the daughters of priests (Leviticus 21:9). This may be good evidence of Tamar's priestly heritage. Even though she has lived at the house of her father while waiting for Shelah to grow up, Tamar still falls under Judah's patriarchal authority. According to the laws of that time, the patriarch of a family had recourse to enforce capital punishment for certain crimes against the family.[14]

Tamar is brought out for execution, but she still has one more card to play before this game is over, and she turns the tables. She coyly says, "By the man, whose these are, am I with child: and she said, Discern, I pray thee, whose are these, the signet, and bracelets, and staff" (38:25). All of these items belong to Judah, and they identify the father of the child without question. With that, the accused Tamar is exonerated and the charges and death sentence against her are dropped.

Judah's next statement is telling. Historically, many translations of Genesis 38:26 render Judah's speech as "She is more righteous than I." This wording makes Judah's acknowledgment a *relative* statement in which he takes the majority of the blame while Tamar still bears part of it. However, modern Bible scholars have derived a more accurate translation in which Judah takes *total* blame and not only exonerates Tamar but expresses *praise* for her: "She is righteous, not I."[15] In this equally viable interpretation, Tamar is completely vindicated and pronounced righteous. This is a defining moment for Judah. He finally realizes what Tamar's intentions were. He sees that she has not been seeking to humiliate him or just been desperate for a child. Such behavior would not merit the term "righteous." He sees that something more profound drove her to take such drastic measures.

Tamar is an *ezer*, a *savior*, of the genealogical line of her husbands. She risks her life and reputation to preserve the family honor. She regards her husbands' seed as sacred and is willing to put her life on the line to save it. When she gives birth to twin sons, she rescues *both* her husbands, Er and Onan, although they do not deserve it. Twice the narrator of Genesis 38 tells us that what these two sons did was "wicked in the Lord's sight." Twice he tells how God acted peremptorily to prevent this wickedness. But the narrator is silent in assigning blame to Tamar. Tamar is righteous, and the men of Judah's household are not.

Even though Tamar has cozened Judah at the crossroads and exposed him to public disgrace, she calls forth his strongest character trait—his sense of decency. He does not deny the truth, make excuses, or place the blame on Tamar. For once, he takes responsibility and places the blame on himself. His behavior foreshadows the great Israelite leader he will become. He has disregarded the law by not providing for Tamar and has disregarded his obligations by sending her away from the family. Yet, ultimately, he shows his upright spirit by acknowledging that he has mistreated her.

Judah's encounter with Tamar profoundly changes him. He had left his brethren in Hebron and gone to live with the Canaanites. He had harbored resentment and jealousy toward the brothers he perceived as being "favored" by his father, Jacob. He initiated the plan to sell Joseph into slavery. But we see the evidence of his change later in Genesis when he travels with his brothers to Egypt to seek relief from the famine. When Benjamin's life is threatened, he volunteers to die in his place. He—the brother who felt he had been passed up—is now offering himself to die in place of his father's darling.[16] Ultimately, Jacob identifies Judah as the leader of his brothers. He prophesies that "the sceptre shall not depart from Judah," and "thy father's children shall bow down before thee" (Genesis 49:10, 8).

Tamar epitomizes women who are victimized by legal or patriarchal systems. Many women today get lost in the red tape of bureaucracy. Tamar has the law on her side, but only extraordinary circumstances allow her to claim her rights. She is a woman who has fallen through the cracks in the law. The law that should protect her traps her instead. She is neither an independent widow nor a married wife. She is a victim of the disobedience of others. She knows that the lives of her future children are more important than the law, and the law must promote life and justice. She has but one right—to be given in marriage according to the levirate law. She depends on that right to save her. She pushes Judah to acknowledge that he is breaking the law and to admit that he knows he is treating her unjustly. She takes a risk and uses an ingenious plan to force the issue.[17]

Through Pharez, her firstborn, Tamar becomes a matriarch in the house of Israel. She becomes a many-times-great-grandmother to Jesus of Nazareth. Many have wondered why a woman such as Tamar is listed in the genealogy of Jesus. A *prostitute* in Jesus's family line? Why does she have to be included? But Tamar did not tarnish the line of Christ. She acted as an *ezer* and rescued it. She used ingenuity and decisive action to bring about justice and righteousness—fairness and human dignity. Of course, her methods would not work in today's world, but modern women can take a lesson from Tamar. They can seek to emulate her strength and assertiveness in bringing about righteousness, not only for themselves but also for their families, their tribes, and their nations. Tamar's courageous actions led her family back into God's covenant. She used her shrewdness and artfulness to bring about the cause of justice in a patriarchal society. In such a society, women could normally bring about change only through their dealings with men. Women like Tamar are remembered for their nonconformity to the unfortunate pattern so commonly seen in the Old Testament—women being passive bystanders while life happens around them and being acted *upon* but are not acting themselves.

Tamar is a wonderful role model for women in every age to use their strength to stand up for what is right, even when they confront powerful obstacles. Tamar stands up to the most powerful man in her life—her father-in-law and the patriarch of the tribe. He has the authority to tell her whom to marry and where to live. He can sentence her to death and not be accountable to anyone. Tamar teaches Judah that "might does not make right." She teaches him what it means to honorably live up to your responsibilities. He becomes a much better man because of Tamar. She *rescues* him from himself. Tamar's life can teach us a great deal about the realities of betrayal and the risks involved in making a difference. She inspires us to question the status quo and to work toward justice.

Tamar is rightly included in the genealogy of Jesus. She shows us that even perceived wrongdoing is redeemable through the Atonement of Jesus. She has much in common with Mary, the mother of Jesus. Tamar, like Mary, is a woman who is pregnant, unmarried, alone, and in peril with the law. She can be killed if no one accepts responsibility for her and her unborn child. Mary must rely on the righteousness of Joseph for her very life as well as that of her child. Tamar holds out the hope that Judah will recognize his hypocrisy and do the right thing. Mary and Tamar both give birth out of the ordinary pattern of their societies. Ultimately, the Lord will protect the women and their children.[18]

Tamar survives the death of two husbands, the disgrace of barrenness, betrayal by her father-in-law, and near death by burning only to emerge triumphant in getting what is rightfully hers. She refuses to wallow in self-pity or accept the injustice dealt to her. Praised for her righteousness, courage, resilience, and skillful manipulation of events, she works within the limitations of the patriarchal system that is responsible for her plight to achieve justice. She is an *ezer* who rescues the family line from extinction and Judah from hypocrisy through her righteousness and resourcefulness.[19] She proves that a single human being can make a difference by using imagination and ingenuity to control her own destiny and the destiny of her descendants.

Notes

1. The book of Jubilees in the *Old Testament Pseudepigrapha* states that Er "hated (her) and would not lie with her because his mother was from the daughters of Canaan. And he wanted to take a wife from his mother's people, but Judah, his father, would not permit him" (Jubilees 41:2–3). Orville S. Wintermute, "Jubilees," *Old Testament Pseudepigrapha*, vol. 2. Edited by James H. Charlesworth (Garden City: Doubleday, 1985), 130.

2. Many scholars assume that Tamar is a Canaanite because no Israelite connection is specified. However, since Judah's wife is specifically referred to as a Canaanite, it could also be argued that since Tamar's ethnicity is not specified, the silence of the text implies she is an Israelite.

3. J. W. Etheridge, *The Targums of Onkelos and Jonathan ben Uzziel on the Pentateuch*, Genesis and Exodus (London: Longman, Green, Longman, and Roberts, 1862), 291.

4. Middle Assyrian Law A 33, in *Ancient Near Eastern Texts Relating to the Old*

Testament. Edited by James B. Prichard (Princeton, New Jersey: Princeton University Press, 1969), 182.

5. James Baker, *Women's Rights in Old Testament Times* (Salt Lake City, Utah: Signature Books, 1992), 150.

6. T. J. Wray, *Good Girls, Bad Girls* (Lanham: Rowman & Littlefield Publishers, 2008) 108.

7. Baker, *Women's Rights in Old Testament Times*, 158, footnote 31.

8. Carolyn Curtis James, *Lost Women of the Bible* (Grand Rapids: Zondervan, 2005), 111.

9. Leila Leah Bronner writes that, "Ironically, Shelah, whose name means 'hers,' is never rightfully given in marriage to Tamar. Shelah never becomes 'hers' because his father fears that he will die like his two older brothers." See Bronner, *Stories of Biblical Mothers: Maternal Power in the Hebrew Bible* (Lanham: University Press of America, 2004), 101.

10. According to Pseudo-Philo in the Pseudepigrapha, Tamar's "intent was not fornication, but being unwilling to separate from the sons of Israel she reflected and said, 'It is better for me to die for having intercourse with my father-in-law than to have intercourse with gentiles' " (9:5).

See D. J. Harrington, "Pseudo-Philo" in *The Old Testament Pseudepigrapha,* vol. 1. Edited by James H. Charlesworth. (Garden City: Doubleday & Co., 1985), 315.

11. Scholar Michael C. Astour has written, "It is known that feasts of the pre-exilic period were accompanied by ritual fornication with the magic intention of securing rich crops and increase of herds. Judah's visit to a hierodule at that time of year was a predictable, ritually prescribed act." See Astour, "Tamar the Hierodule" in *Journal for Biblical Literature.* 85 (1966), 193.

12. Megan McKenna, *Not Counting Women and Children* (Maryknoll: Orbis Books, 1994), 96.

13. In the Bible, Tamar was to be burned because she was a harlot. Jubilees, which was written much later than Genesis, emphasizes the prohibition against intimate sexual relations between fathers-in-law and daughters-in-law. It states that Judah was forgiven because he committed the sin unknowingly and that he repented, having "gone astray because he uncovered the robe of his son." He "condemned himself in his own sight." He is told in a dream by the Lord that "it was forgiven him because he made a great supplication and because he mourned and did not do it again." See Jubilees 41:23–24 in *The Old Testament Pseudepigrapha*, vol. 2. Edited by Charlesworth, 131.

14. Baker, *Women's Rights in Old Testament Times*, 152 and footnote 35.

15. The preposition *min* in Hebrew can be viewed as a "comparative of exclusion," in which the subject alone bears the quality described. Only Tamar is righteous, not Judah. The Hebrew is ambiguous here. See Bruce K. Waltke, *Genesis: A Commentary* (Grand Rapids: Zondervan, 2001), 513.

See also Bruce K. Waltke and M. O'Connor, *An Introduction to Biblical Hebrew Syntax*, (Winona Lake: Eisenbrauns, 1990), 265; and *Gesenius' Hebrew Grammar*. Edited by E. Kautzsch (London: Oxford University Press, 1910), 430, footnote 2.

16. James, *Lost Women of the Bible*, 116.
17. McKenna, *Not Counting Women and Children*, 98.
18. Ibid., 98–99.
19. Wray, *Good Girls, Bad Girls*, 108–109.

Conclusion

PERHAPS THE BEST WAY TO measure these forgotten women of the scriptures is according to God's purpose for women. Genesis says that God created woman as a companion to man, to be an *ezer*—a strength or power—exactly suited to him. The Hebrew word *ezer* is used in the scriptures to refer to God *delivering* Israel from her enemies, or *rescuing* her from dangerous situations—helping Israel, for example, by raining down hailstones on the heads of opposing armies.

These women are *strong*. They are creative and ingenious in the ways they approach their problems. They refuse to accept the status quo and try to think of solutions that lie within the scope of their power to accomplish. Jael plays the gracious hostess in order to lull a brutal general to his death. She uses the tools she has at hand—a tent peg and some goat's milk—to accomplish her designs. Judith pretends to be willing to cooperate with the enemy and offers to supply him with strategic information. She gains the upper hand by pretending to be weak. Miriam courageously proposes an arrangement to the daughter of Pharaoh that could be dangerous if she does not handle it carefully.

These women are *life-savers*. They *rescue* those around them. Jochebed, the mother of Moses, hides her baby in a reed basket to keep him from becoming a victim of the king's killing edict. Zipporah, the wife of Moses, literally saves Moses' life when God tries to kill him for not circumcising his son. She performs the rite of circumcision on her son with a sharp stone, even though it is an ordinance usually performed by men. Pharaoh's daughter risks her position in the royal court because of her compassion for a Hebrew baby.

These women are *faithful in the face of powerful opposition* and threats to their lives. Shiphrah and Puah defy the edict of the king that commands they kill all the newborn Hebrew male babies. Susanna refuses to submit to the evil elders who threaten to slander her if she does not submit to them. She would rather be destroyed than sin against God. The mother in *4 Maccabees* is dedicated to Jewish piety despite having to endure the greatest torture a mother can suffer—watching her child be tortured and killed. And she does this not just once but *seven* times.

These women *do what needs to be done*. They step up. They don't depend on the people around them to solve their problems. Sitis, the wife of Job, sells her hair to keep Job from starving. Jael and Judith use their feminine wiles to lure powerful men, even generals, to their deaths "at the hand of a woman"—the ultimate disgrace for such men. Tamar desires a child to ensure that her husband's genealogical line is perpetuated. Being deprived of the justice she deserves, she decides to obtain a child by an "alternate method" and pretends to be a harlot. Today, a woman who has been defrauded as Tamar was could appeal to a women's rights advocate and find an attorney to take her case pro bono. But Tamar's social system does not allow that. She has to work within the existing social structure, so she improvises.

These women are an *inspiration to the men around them*. Deborah motivates Barak to lead the armies of Israel against the mighty armies of Sisera. He will not go to battle unless she goes with him. She inspires him to be his strongest self. Sitis inspires her husband Job through her love, compassion, and dedication to him even while he spends years sitting on a dung heap and scraping the pus off his boils. Noah's wife, Naamah, stands by her husband while all the world scorns him and laughs. Tamar inspires Judah to be his best self. She pushes him to recognize that he has wronged her. After being exposed to public disgrace, he shows his sense of decency and acknowledges her righteousness.

These women *cling to God*, even when they are at the end of their ropes. Hannah could easily have given up on God. Her yearly pilgrimages to the temple are sheer torture as she is forced to listen to her co-wife's constant taunts about Hannah's childlessness. But she keeps her faith in God even though she is in near despair. Susanna would rather die than betray her God. Hagar takes solace in knowing that God is the only one who cares that she is miserable. She even names him—"The God Who Sees Me."

These women *exemplify steadfast faithfulness*. Once Aseneth is converted, she fasts and prays for forgiveness of her former idolatry and pledges eternal obedience to the one true God. Hannah tenaciously clings to her faith that God will not leave her destitute, even though she receives no evidence that God will send her a son. Judith remains a pious widow who is loyal to the memory of her husband and her God despite her affluence and opportunities to move in other directions with her life. She believes that God could save her city and refuses to consider surrendering. Deborah judges her people for forty years in righteousness and faith.

These women *sacrifice for the Lord and for those they love*. The mother in *4 Maccabees* encourages her seven sons to remain true to Jewish law even though they are brutally tortured and killed before her eyes. She would rather they remain pious than remain alive. Hannah is willing to sacrifice her only son to the Lord's service in order to show her gratitude to the Lord for answering her prayer. Jephthah's daughter, Seila, willingly sacrifices her opportunity for a life with a husband and children so that her father might honor his vow to God. Hagar heeds the Lord's command to return to her abusive mistress because the Lord asks her to.

These women are faithful no matter what comes their way. These women are us—us at our best.

GLOSSARY

apocrypha

That which is "hidden away" or "concealed." *Apocryphon* is the singular noun and *apocrypha* the plural noun. These words are used to describe the nature of a certain body of ancient religious writings. The word *apocrypha* originally meant "a writing too sacred and secret to be in everyone's hands." It needed to be hidden away and reserved for the spiritually mature. It was a term of dignity and respect. To those who revered the apocryphal books, they were "hidden" because they contained teachings that were too sacred to be revealed except to the initiated.

Babylonian captivity

This term refers to the deportation and exile of the residents of Judah to Babylon in 587 B.C. by Nebuchadnezzar II. It coincided with the destruction of the monarchy and the Temple of Solomon. After the overthrow of Babylon by the Persian Empire, the Persian ruler Cyrus the Great gave the Jews permission to return to their homeland and rebuild the temple in 539 B.C.

Book of Jubilees

Also known as the "Little Genesis" and "The Apocalypse of Moses," the Book of Jubilees is attributed to the very hand of Moses himself. Moses supposedly penned it while he was on Mount Sinai as an angel of God dictated it. The book is told from the viewpoint of the angel himself, and it unfolds heaven's view of history. The text covers the creation of man, as well as Adam's fall from grace, and goes on to fill in many details of Israel's history.

canon

Canon comes from the Hebrew word *kanah*, which means "reed." Reeds were originally used as measuring sticks. Thus, *canon* designates the "standard" or the "rule." Canonical works are those deemed to be reliable as statements of doctrine and faith. Apocryphal literature is therefore called "non-canonical" or "extra-canonical."

extracanonical

Works that are not found within the accepted scriptures of a religion.

Intertestamental period

The period of time between the writings of canonical Old and New Testament texts, spanning the ministry of Malachi and John the Baptist. Traditionally, it is considered to be roughly a four hundred year period. During this time, many non-canonical texts were written

Josephus

A first-century Jewish historian who survived and recorded the destruction of Jerusalem in A.D. 70. His two most important works are *The Jewish War* (c. 75) and *Antiquities of the Jews* (c. 94). *Antiquities of the Jews* recounts the history of the world from a Jewish perspective. His works give important insight into first-century Judaism.

midrash

An ancient commentary on part of the Hebrew scriptures that is based on Jewish methods of interpretation and attached to the biblical text.

Mishnah

The Mishnah is a major work of Rabbinic Judaism, and the first major redaction into written form of Jewish oral traditions, called the Oral Torah.

nazarite

A Jew bound by a vow to leave the hair uncut, to abstain from wine and strong drink, and to practice extraordinary purity and devotion to God. This obligation could be for life or for a limited time. See Numbers 6:2–21.

pseudepigrapha

Texts whose claimed authorship is unfounded and whose real author has attributed it to a figure from the past. *Pseudepigrapha* is from the Greek *pseudes* meaning "false," and *epigraph*, meaning "inscription." Thus, a widely accepted but incorrect attribution of authorship may make a perfectly authentic text pseudepigraphical. In religious studies, the Pseudepigrapha are Jewish works written between 200 B.C. and A.D. 200, not all of which are literally pseudepigraphical.

Pseudo-Philo

The author of the pseudepigraphical work *Biblical Antiquities*. *Biblical Antiquities* is a retelling of the stories in the Old Testament that reflects Jewish legend and tradition as they existed in the first century. The author probably lived in Palestine and wrote in Hebrew.

rabbinic literature

In its broadest sense, rabbinic literature can refer to the entire spectrum of rabbinic writings throughout Jewish history, but the term often refers to literature from the Talmudic era (the first five centuries) as opposed to medieval or modern rabbinic writing.

redaction

In the study of literature, redaction is a form of editing in which multiple source texts are combined together and subjected to minor alteration to make them into a single work. Often this is a method of collecting a series of writings on a similar theme and creating a definitive and coherent work.

Septuagint

The oldest Greek version of the Old Testament, or simply "LXX." It is said that Jewish scholars translated it from the Hebrew at the request of Ptolemy II. The translation was done in Alexandria,

Egypt, and was completed about 250 B.C. Because of the Jewish diaspora, or "scattering," there were thousands of Jews who could no longer read the Hebrew scriptures. This translation was made to accommodate their needs.

Talmud

Talmud is from a Hebrew root which means, "to teach," or "to study." The Talmud is a record of rabbinic discussions pertaining to Jewish law, ethics, customs, and history. Over the centuries, various rabbis transmitted their opinions orally and later recorded them. After the Jewish temple was destroyed in A.D. 70, Judaism faced a crisis. The old system of oral scholarship could not be maintained because the temple no longer existed as a center for learning and discussion. During this period rabbinic discourse began to be recorded in writing. The Babylonian Talmud was compiled around 500 A.D. The Jerusalem Talmud predates its counterpart by two hundred years.

Targum

When the Jews returned to Jerusalem to rebuild their temple after the Babylonian captivity, they spoke the *lingua franca* of Babylon, which was Aramaic. Although Aramaic was a cousin to Hebrew, they could no longer understand the Hebrew scriptures when the scribes read them aloud. The scribes had to explain the meaning of the Hebrew words to the people, and their interpretations reflect the way the scriptures were understood at the time. These explanations were called Targums, and were written down and collected during the following centuries.

Torah

Torah means "the Law," and it includes the first five books of Moses—Genesis, Exodus, Leviticus, Numbers, and Deuteronomy.

About the Author

Diana Webb was born and raised in Salt Lake City, Utah. She graduated magna cum laude from the University of Utah in 1972 with a degree in English education. She taught at John F. Kennedy Junior High for two years before serving an LDS mission in Hong Kong, where she learned to speak Cantonese. Afterward, she taught at Northwest Intermediate School.

She met and married Randy Webb while he was in dental school in San Francisco. They were married in the Salt Lake Temple and have three children and six grandchildren.

In 1993, Diana decided to earn her masters degree at Brigham Young University in Ancient Near Eastern studies. With the help of a tutor, she polished up her twenty-five-year-old math skills, took the GRE, and became a coed again at age forty-three. She sent the kids off to school, popped a frozen casserole in the oven on timed bake, and drove to BYU every day. She finished her degree in one year, writing a thesis titled, "A Portrayal of the Matriarchs in the Old Testament Pseudepigrapha." After graduation in 1994, she started teaching at Salt Lake Community College's Institute of Religion. In 2006 she transferred to LDS Business College, where she continues to teach.

Diana also enjoys watercolor painting. She has even won a couple of ribbons at the Utah State Fair. Her other hobbies include scrapbooking, reading, sewing, attending plays, shopping, and researching family history. In 2008 she finished a 366-page family history on her Barton ancestors, which took her three years to complete. She has also written and illustrated a children's book about one of her ancestors.